P9-DHE-689

Rupert's
FORT VANCOUVER
PORTLAND
COLUMBIA RIVER
OREGON COUNTRY
WAIILATPU
FORT BOISE
OREGON
SNAKE RIVER
FORT HALL
GREAT SALT LAKE
SOUTH PASS
SCOTT'S BLUFF
FORT LARAMIE
MEXICO
DISPUTED AREA
CHIMNEY ROCK
PLATTE RIVER
MISSOURI RIVER
UNORGANIZED TERRITORY
TRAIL
IOWA TERRITORY 1838
WISCONSIN TERRITORY 1836
MISSISSIPPI RIVER
FORT DEARBORN (CHICAGO)
LAKE
NAUVOO
Illinois
NEW SALEM
INDEPENDENCE
SANTA FE TRAIL
HANNIBAL
SPRINGFIELD
WABASH RIVER
Indiana
ST. LOUIS
VANDALIA
The NATIONAL ROAD
COLUMB
Missouri
ARKANSAS RIVER
REPUBLIC OF TEXAS
CAVE-IN-ROCK
CINCINNATI
EULA
OHIO RIVER
Arkansas 1836
Kentucky
LEXINGTON
NASHVILLE
WILDERNESS ROAD
NATCHEZ TRACE
Tennessee
Cumberland Gap

The Tragic Tale of

NARCISSA WHITMAN

and a Faithful History of the
☞ OREGON TRAIL ☜

PAINSTAKINGLY WRITTEN AND ILLUSTRATED BY

CHERYL HARNESS

NATIONAL GEOGRAPHIC
WASHINGTON, D.C.

*"To be at a distance
and hear [the Indians] singing...,
one would almost forget he
was in a savage land."*

— Narcissa Whitman
Waiilatpu Mission
May 2, 1837

Contents

THE OREGON TRAIL
1836

FORT WALLA WALLA
FORT VANCOUVER
SOUTH PASS
FORT LARAMIE
ANGELICA N.Y.
LIBERTY
ST. LOUIS
MEXICO
Rendezvous

Narcissa Whitman

JUST THINK OF IT: Back in the 20th century, a little over 65 years passed between the Wright Brothers' 1903 flight and the astronauts' 1969 moonwalk. Every bit as amazing was the 19th century's huge westward techno-leap. Less than 63 years after Lewis and Clark returned from their epic trek in 1806, the United States was coast-to-coast connected with stagecoaches, telegraph wires, and a transcontinental railroad.

One of the most famous stories of those pioneer days was the sad tale of Narcissa Whitman. Why? Because when she and Eliza Spalding went West in 1836, they represented everything civilized back in the States. If a couple of white ladies – Narcissa and Eliza were the first – could get out to Oregon on their sidesaddles, it meant that families, schools, churches, and towns would soon follow. The Indians of the West would be shoved out of the way just as those in the East had been. Americans were on the same old collision course they'd been on since colonial days.

Narcissa Prentiss Whitman symbolizes the bitter and the sweet of East meeting West, of settler meeting Indian. She represents a time when thousands of Americans, loaded down, then as now, with hopes, good intentions, fears, and misunderstandings, set out on the great and perilous Oregon Trail.

When
NARCISSA PRENTISS WHITMAN
came into the world
1808

"Whatever shall we do in that remote spot?"
Napoleon I
(1769–1821)

THOS. JEFFERSON

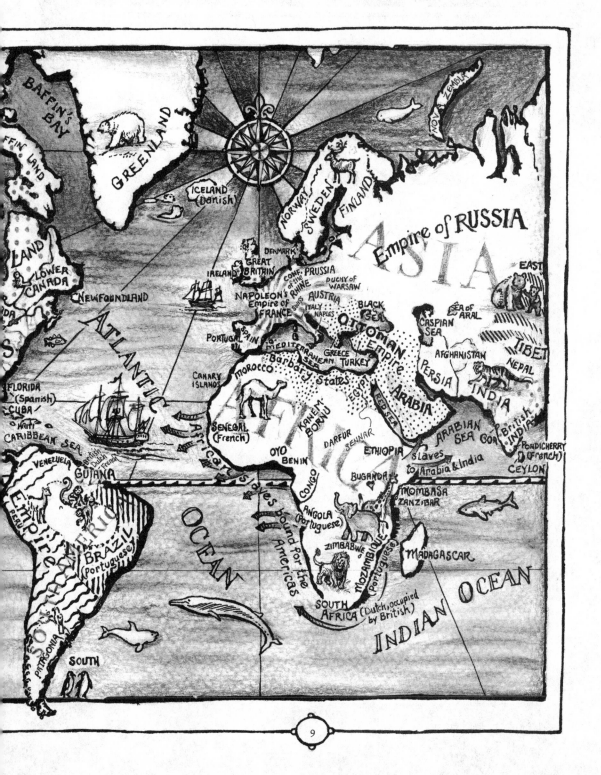

CHAPTER ONE

Over the River and Through the Mountains

WESTWARD

NARCISSA PRENTISS WHITMAN NEVER INTENDED to be a poster girl for her country's westward movement, but that sure is part of what she became. So before you learn about her, it'd be a good thing for you to know about what was going on in America before she came on the scene.

For centuries, whether they were climbing aboard the *Mayflower* or following Daniel Boone down the Wilderness Road, folks had gone questing for their hearts' desires out where few had gone, on the far frontier. For Europeans in the 1600s, that

1808   *Note: The time line features events that took place around the world during Narcissa's lifetime.*

Italy —
Archeological excavations are going on at Pompeii, the town destroyed by the volcano Vesuvius, 79 A.D.

Mahmud II *is new sultan of the Ottoman Empire.*

September 8 —
Osage Indians sign away their lands in Missouri and Arkansas. They'll move to a reservation in present-day Oklahoma.

land of dreams was on the Atlantic Ocean's wild and distant shore, future home of England's 13 Colonies. For Americans in the 1700s, the frontier lay on the sundown side of the Appalachian Mountains. Then, all through the 1800s, it kept right on moving a step ahead of the people, across the Mississippi, the prairie, the plains, over and through the Rockies, Cascades, and Sierras, as pioneers pushed on, on, and on, risking everything to find a better kind of life.

Some looked for a life in which they could pray as they saw fit without being thrown in jail. Some daring souls wanted to see for themselves if they had the faith and guts it took to survive what — or who — they might find out there. People felt pushed by what they wanted to get away from. They were pulled by what they wanted to find: New land for the nation. New souls for God. Furs. Gold. Adventure. A waterway through North America to the Pacific Ocean and on to the wealthy marketplaces of Asia. Some who went, kids, for instance, had no choice. Some folks just couldn't stand being left behind. Oh, to start life over again somewhere else! And which way did almost every single one of these folks go? West.

It'd be hard to pick an exact time-and-space intersection when America's westward migration began. After men planted

---

1808

December 22 —
Austrian concert-goers hear the world's first performance of **Ludwig van Beethoven**'s 5th and 6th Symphonies. They're not impressed.

1809

January 4 —
Louis Braille, inventor of a reading method for the blind, is born in France.

January 19 —
Boston, MA —
Edgar Allan Poe, author, is born on **General Robert E. Lee**'s 2nd birthday.

themselves at Jamestown, Virginia, in 1607, it took a little over 150 years for folks to chop, plow, and build their way across the land between the Atlantic coast and the Appalachians.

Just as the War for Independence was beginning in 1775, Daniel Boone and his axmen hacked open a trail so families could get themselves, their beasts, and their wagons through the Cumberland Gap and into the wilds of Kentucky and Tennessee. In 1787, the birth year of the U.S. Constitution, settlers struggled into the Northwest Territory, lands which would be Ohio and four other states plus a bit of Minnesota. Then the Americans of 1803 tried to imagine 827,987 square miles of wilderness, bought with their tax money from the emperor of France. What in the world might there be out in that Louisiana Purchase over on the other side of the Mississippi River? The finding out began in the spring of 1804, when explorers set off, waving farewells to the folks around St. Louis. Not until late 1806 would they see each other again.

From the lowest apprentice to President Jefferson, Americans had waited two years for news of the explorers. At last, here they were: Captain Meriwether Lewis, Captain William Clark, and their band of iron-muscled, hard-tested explorers. They'd traveled to the Pacific Ocean and back, and all but one of them lived to tell the tale.

February 3 —
Jakob Ludwig Felix Mendelssohn, *composer, is born in Germany.*

February 12 —
Abraham Lincoln, *16th president, is born in Kentucky.*
Charles Darwin, *naturalist, is born in England.*

March 4 —
James Madison *becomes the 4th president.*

June 8 —
Thomas Paine, *author/ patriot, dies in New York.*

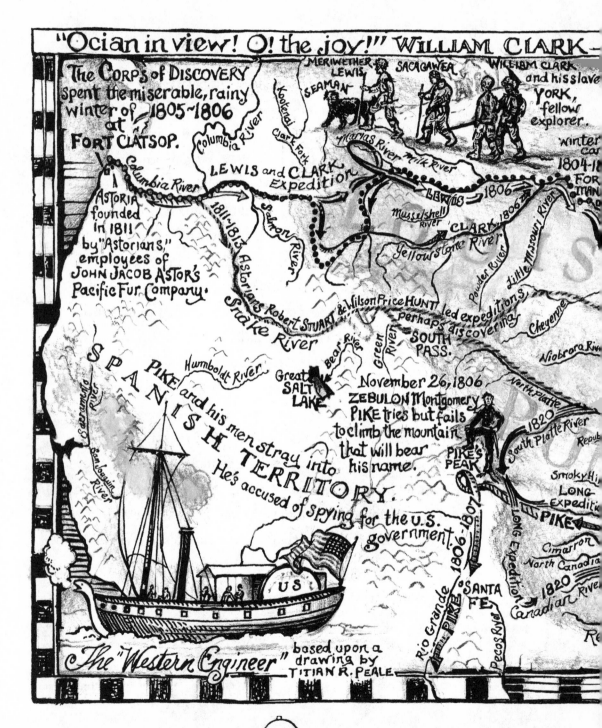

"Ocian in view! O! the joy!" WILLIAM CLARK

The Corps of Discovery spent the miserable, rainy winter of 1805~1806 at FORT CLATSOP.

MERIWETHER LEWIS

SACAGAWEA

WILLIAM CLARK and his slave YORK, fellow explorer.

SEAMAN

Columbia River

Kootenai River

Clark Fork

LEWIS and CLARK Expedition

Marias River

Milk River

LEWIS 1806

winter ca 1804-18 FOR MAN D

A Astoria founded in 1811 by "Astorians," employees of JOHN JACOB ASTOR'S Pacific Fur Company.

Columbia River

1811-1815 Astorians Robert Stuart

Salmon River

Musselshell River

CLARK 1806

Little Missouri River

Yellowstone River

Powder River

& Wilson Price HUNT led expeditions, perhaps discovering SOUTH PASS.

Snake River

Cheyenne

Niobrara River

Bear River

Green River

S P A N I S H   T E R R I T O R Y.

Humboldt River

Great SALT LAKE

November 26, 1806 ZEBULON Montgomery PIKE tries but fails to climb the mountain that will bear his name.

North Platte

1820

South Platte River

Repub

Sacramento River

PIKE and his men stray into

He's accused of spying for the U.S. government.

PIKE'S PEAK

Smoky Hi LONG Expediti

San Joaquin River

Long Expedition

PIKE

PIKE 1806-1807

US

Cimarron North Canadian

1820 Canadian River

Rio Grande

°SANTA FE.

Pecos River

Re

The "Western Engineer" based upon a drawing by TITIAN R. PEALE

THE EXPLORERS

It was going to take more than the heroic captains and their sturdy bunch to comprehend and map the wilds beyond the Mississippi River. In 1806, when Lewis and Clark's Corps of Discovery was still working its way back from the Pacific Ocean, the hard-luck explorer Zebulon Pike was setting off to discover what lay along the uncertain southern border of the Louisiana Purchase territory. As it turned out, he and his suffering men were captured by Spanish soldiers and taken deep into modern-day Mexico before they were finally released. Pike brought back many observations, including his sighting of a particular peak on the Front Range of the Rocky Mountains. It was a later explorer, Stephen H. Long, who named it Pike's Peak. Between the years 1817 and 1823, he and other scientific observers adventured into the Rocky Mountains and lands along the Platte, the Red, and the Mississippi Rivers. On his 1819–20 expedition, Long and his companions went up the Missouri aboard a steamboat, the *Western Engineer*. Some called it "Long's Dragon" because of the way engine smoke poured out of its serpent-headed bow. A sensational sight it must have been for the natives living along the river.

BEAVER HATS

NO WAGON TRAINS WOULD BE ROLLING in the footsteps of Lewis and Clark. Much of their route was too bumpy and dangerous. The explorers hadn't found the long-searched-for waterway to the Pacific Ocean either, but, oh boy, what they did find! People, plants and animals, and mountain streams bristling with *Castor canadensis*: beavers. And wherever these toothy dam builders were, there was money to be made. Their glossy pelts were as good as gold.

Since the 1500s, fur trapping and trading had been the main money-making industries in North America for Indians and Europeans. They had helped keep the Plymouth colonists alive in the early 1600s. In the 1700s, competition for furs led, in part, to the French and Indian War. Since the earliest times, people have needed other creatures' skins in order to keep warm, but it was the

1809

July —
Tecumseh *and his brother* **Tenskwatawa, the Shawnee Prophet,** *begin organizing the tribes east of the Rocky Mountains to fight off invading white settlers.*

October 11 —
Explorer **Meriwether Lewis,** 35, *dies in Tennessee.*

Ecuador wins independence from Spain.

desire for a fine-looking hat that really turbo-charged the fur trade. Just about everyone wore hats.

Now, don't be picturing beavers on people's heads. Their hats were made of felt, a kind of thick fabric made from fur or

Saying "hello" in a world full of hats

wool. Felt was made like this: Once the skin was parted from the animal who'd gone around living in it, a hatter would remove the *guard hairs* (the outer fur). Underneath was the valuable layer of furry insulation, which kept the animal warm and dry. This the hatter shaved away, then he'd stir these underfur fibers, dampen, press, squeeze, and beat them into felt, which would be made into hats. Any fur would do—otter, muskrat, seal, rabbit—but most prized was that of the glossy beaver. The animal might have been trapped

1810

Maryland — **Elizabeth Seton** *establishes the Sisters of Charity of St. Joseph, founders of orphanages, schools, and hospitals.*

September 15–16 — Dolores, Mexico — **Father Miguel Hidalgo y Costilla** *begins Mexico's war for independence. He raises up an army of peasants against their Spanish rulers (see 1811).*

U.S. population: 7,215,858

First world globes made in the U.S.A. are crafted by **James Wilson** *of Vermont.*

into extinction if, in the 1830s, shiny silk hats hadn't come along.

Meanwhile, back in the first years of the 19th century, streams in the 15 U.S. states were becoming trapped out, beaverless. The powerful English Hudson Bay Company and its Canadian competitor, the Northwest Company, were mapping and trapping the wilds of Canada clear out to the Pacific Coast, down into the Oregon Country. Their fur hunters were a hardy bunch of French Canadians and Iroquois men, as well as Indian slaves, male and female, captured in battles and village raids.

Hard-headed businessmen, such as Manuel Lisa, the Chouteau brothers, German immigrant John Jacob Astor, and others, scrambled to set up fur trading posts in the wilderness described by Captains Lewis and Clark. And a rough business it was, too. No trail tale can be told without the generation of men who took up their traps and dared all sorts of dangers as they scoured western America for pelts. As they did, these frontiersmen learned the paths and passages through the wilderness. Hundreds of thousands of folks and their animals would follow these and create the Oregon Trail. But they'd be coming along later, off in the future. It's 1808 now. Another sort of trailblazer is about to enter the world's stage.

1810

A large comet is seen
in the sky this year.

France —
Nicholas Appert *publishes the
method he invented for canning
and preserving food.*

March 1 — Poland —
Frederic Chopin, *composer, is born.*

July 5 —
Phineas T. Barnum, *showman,
circus owner, is born in Connecticut.*

NARCISSA

IN THE VILLAGE OF PRATTSBURG, out in wild, western New York, Clarissa Prentiss, the carpenter's wife, had a baby — a sister for their two little boys. Over the next 12 years, Clarissa and her husband, Stephen, a big, tall, serious pair, would have baby Jonas, then Jane, Mary Ann, Clarissa, Harriet, and Edward. But for the time being, as of Monday, March 14, 1808, the Prentiss family numbered five: father, mother, Stephen Jr., Harvey, and new baby Narcissa.

What's going on in this baby's world? The Earth's human population has reached one billion, one sixth of where we are now. Of that number, a little over five million are living in the United States. The sun is just coming up on the Industrial Age. Inventors Robert Fulton and Richard Trevithick have been doing cutting-edge experiments with steam-powered boats and trains. More and more African territory is and will be grabbed up

1811

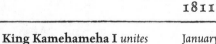

King Kamehameha I *unites the Hawaiian Islands, a.k.a. the Sandwich Islands.* **Captain James Cook** *named them in 1778 after the Earl of Sandwich, his boss at the English admiralty.*

January 8–10 — Louisiana — Enslaved people rise up against their owners. As many as a hundred slaves are killed when the rebellion is crushed.

by European powers. Around the eastern coast of the Mediterranean Sea, the Islamic Ottoman Empire is slowly losing its power and influence. France is still recovering from its bloody Revolution. Still, her charismatic emperor, Napoleon Bonaparte, is doing a pretty good and frightening job of conquering Europe.

President Thomas Jefferson, in his last year in office, is anxious to get back to working on Monticello, his remarkable hilltop house in Virginia. As of 1800, there are nearly 900,000 black slaves in the United States. Now, in 1808, the Congress has just made a law against bringing any more Africans to be enslaved in the "sweet land of liberty," as America will be called in a song one day, known by its first line: "My country 'tis of thee." Samuel Smith, who'll grow up to write those words, is born in Boston this year, when Narcissa is seven months old.

Off north a ways from the Prentiss house, in Federal Hollow (known as Rushville, later on), a little boy might be tagging along after his big brother, Augustus, or helping their folks, Beza and Alice, with the chores. In any case, five-year-old Marcus Whitman certainly has no idea and probably would wrinkled his nose if you told him that Narcissa Prentiss, his future wife, has just been born.

1811

Industrial Revolution Revolt — English "Luddites" protest low pay, long hours, and brutal conditions in the cloth factories by organizing, rioting, and trying to wreck the weaving machines.

*Because 73-year-old **King George III** has become insane, the Prince of Wales will rule England now as regent.*

She grew up in a very religious household. On Sundays, Mrs. Prentiss made sure her family prayed together before they went off to church for more prayers, a long sermon, and hymns. Blond-headed Narcissa loved the singing. As she grew up, folks admired her voice. And, unlike her parents, she was known to laugh — not in church though! Narcissa's mom was a very strict Presbyterian, and her discipline was firm.

After more church in the afternoon, they could do nice, quiet, things like walk by the stream that wound its way through the village. Even on Sundays the stream turned the waterwheel that ran Mr. Prentiss's mills, where his boys helped saw logs into boards and grind wheat into flour. Narcissa's dad ran a distillery, too, where corn and rye were turned into whiskey. This got him into trouble sometimes, when the church folk got fired up against drinking.

Of course, Sunday afternoons were dandy for reading. Narcissa liked learning about heroic men and their wives who risked terrible dangers, bringing Christian ideas and, by the way, western culture to the *heathens* (seemingly uncivilized people without religion) in Asia and the Pacific islands and to the Jews and Muslims of Palestine.

July 30 — Mexico — The Spanish authorities execute priest **Miguel Hidalgo y Costilla** for stirring up the people's demands for independence.

October 22 — **Franz Liszt**, *pianist, composer, is born in Hungary.*

The men of **John Jacob Astor**'s *Pacific Fur Company establish a trading post, Astoria, at the mouth of the Columbia River.*

To young Narcissa Prentiss, missionaries were celebrities. Their lives were so much more exotic and adventurous than life in her little town. Her mom led meetings of the Female Home Missionary Society right in the Prentisses' parlor. Ladies sipped tea and planned how to raise funds for the missions so that unenlightened foreigners could read the Bible, learn about the civilized life, and have their souls saved from a fiery forever in the afterlife. Such noble goals were worth praying for and dropping dimes into the offering plate. So said many a preacher before serving up a hot sermon to plenty of folks like Narcissa Prentiss, who took her religion strong and life seriously. In her world, so many people were flocking to church that this time in America is called the second Great Awakening. The first was back in the early 1700s when Benjamin Franklin was a young man.

Narcissa's dad helped to drum up money for Prattsburg's boys-only secondary school, Franklin Academy. Teenage Narcissa went there, too, when it added classes for females in 1827. She might also have studied for a while at Mrs. Willard's Female Seminary.

Unlike most people in this time in the world, Emma Hart Willard believed that young women should be allowed to study more than literature, music, and needlework — subjects thought

1811

Haiti —
Ex-slave **Henri Christophe** *is crowned king.*

*November 7 —
Indiana Territory —*
William Henry Harrison *and 6,000 fighters defeat native warriors led by the* **Shawnee Prophet** *in the Battle of Tippecanoe (see 1841).*

First steamboat on the Mississippi River! **Nicholas and Lydia Roosevelt** *and their dog ride* **Robert Fulton's** *paddlewheeler south to New Orleans.*

to be more ladylike. She insisted upon teaching geometry, history, geography, sciences, Latin, and Greek. Thousands of future teachers and at least one future revolutionary, Elizabeth Cady Stanton, would study at Mrs. Willard's school. It was located in Troy, New York, at the eastern end of the newly completed engineering marvel: the Erie Canal.

The Erie Canal, the amazing, impossible water highway

This 40-foot-wide, 4-foot-deep, 363 miles of stone-lined boatway threaded its way through locks and low bridges from the Great Lakes to the Hudson River, which flowed on down to New York City and the Atlantic Ocean. Loads of folks and their goods piled onto the slender canal boats and barges. Many a traveler used this amazing "ditch" for their migration into Pennsylvania and beyond.

November 20 — Cumberland, MD — Work begins on the Great National Pike. In time, gut-shaking stagecoaches will be rattling down this bumpy "National" or "Cumberland" Road clear out to Vandalia, IL.

December 16 — The Mississippi River flows backward from the force of the New Madrid earthquake — one of the nation's worst ever — at Missouri's boot heel.

Jane Austen *writes* Sense and Sensibility.

Life was changing fast. Wider and wider, the doorways to the West were opening. More and more, folks were learning what was out there. Traders, with their mules and oxen, had begun traipsing down the Santa Fe Trail. In February 1822, when Narcissa was 13, William H. Ashley and Andrew Henry, a pair of St. Louis merchants, advertised for a hundred "Enterprising Young Men" to hunt the American Northwest for furs. The fellows who showed up over the next few years would come to be known as "mountain men," frontier legends in their own time.

Back East, far from the wild frontier, another sort of enterprising young man showed up in Narcissa's life. Henry Spalding, who hoped to be a preacher, asked her to marry him, but she said no. Being the wife of intense, awkward Mr. Spalding wasn't Narcissa's idea of a dream-come-true. No, she would teach. It was a proper profession, but really she had another ambition in mind.

"I frequently desired to go to the heathen," wrote 16-year-old Narcissa, in a letter to the American Board of Commissioners of Foreign Missions, "but only half-heartedly and it was not until the first Monday of Jan. 1824 that I felt to consecrate myself without reserve to the Missionary work."

1812

Jakob and **Wilhelm Grimm** *write their Fairy Tales.*

February 7 — **Charles Dickens,** *author, is born in England.*

April 30 — *Louisiana becomes the 18th state.*

June 1 — *The U.S., fed up with British bullying on the high seas, declares war. The War of 1812 begins.*

Napoleon's *French empire covers most of Europe. Now his 600,000 soldiers invade Russia. Getting out won't be so easy.*

"I frequently desired to go to the heathen..."

Young Narcissa imagines a future for herself.

True, the Board had sent a very few single ladies off to be missionaries. What Narcissa really hoped was that God would send her a better job offer: Missionary Wife. What neither she nor the rest of her world of church folks were planning on was the personally delivered bombshell from the far side of the Rocky Mountains.

1813

Winter —
Fleeing Russians set fire to Moscow. Half a million freezing, starving French soldiers die in the snow as **Napoleon**'s army retreats from Russia.

War of 1812 updates — **General Zebulon Pike,** former explorer, is killed as American troops capture York (Toronto), Canada.

British troops burn Buffalo, NY, and capture Fort Niagara. American forces take Fort St. George.

At Lake Erie, **Oliver Hazzard Perry**'s U.S. fleet defeats British warships.

to the Gila in Mexico, the beaver hunter has set his traps in every creek and stream

MOUNTAIN MEN

In truth, the enterprising fellows who went fur-questing in the West were often broke, lonesome, and mighty uncomfortable. Hugh Glass, for instance, survived a bear-attack and desperate cross-country crawl. Still, stacks of books are stuffed with the adventures of such men as Joe Meek and African-American Moses "Black" Harris. Around many a campfire, folks talked about the bragging old drunkard of a riverman-turned-trapper, Mike Fink, the Sublette brothers, Jim Clyman, and Jim Beckwourth, child of a Virginia slave and her white owner.

Before Comanche warriors killed him down on the Santa Fe Trail, Jedediah Smith made epic journeys through the Southwest and up into the Oregon Country, carrying a big knife in his belt and a Bible in his bedroll.

An illiterate teenager when he started out, Jim Bridger came to be known as the King of the Mountain Men for the wealth of frontier lore he carried behind his weathered face. Sure, these tough guys brought piles of pelts out of the far country, but even more valuable was their knowledge of the West. In the early days of America's westward movement, mountain men led the way.

"From the Mississippi to the mouth of the Colorado of the West, from the frozen regions of the North

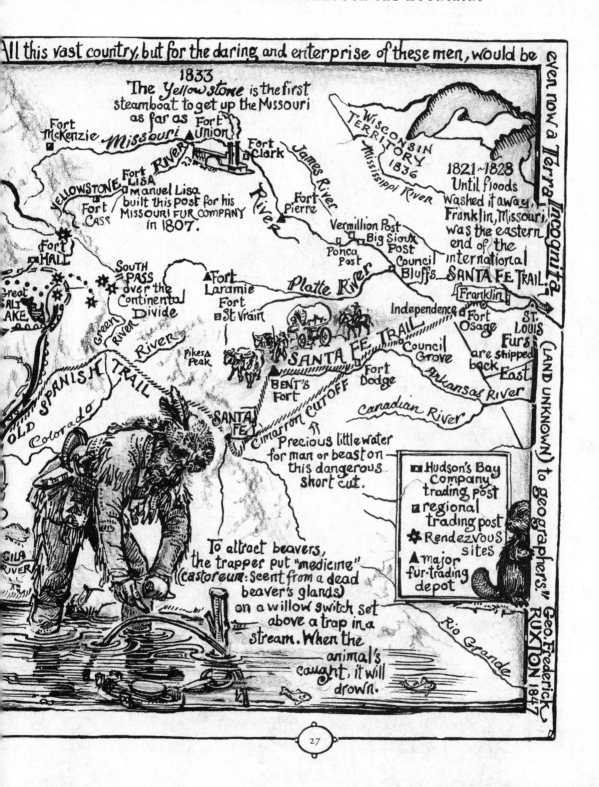

All this vast country, but for the daring and enterprise of these men, would be even now a Terra Incognita (LAND UNKNOWN) to geographers." Geo. Frederick RUXTON 1847

1833
The *Yellowstone* is the first steamboat to get up the Missouri as far as Fort Union

Fort McKenzie

Missouri River

Fort Clark

WISCONSIN TERRITORY 1836

Mississippi River

1821~1828
Until floods washed it away, Franklin, Missouri, was the eastern end of the international SANTA FE TRAIL.

Fort Lisa
Manuel Lisa built this post for his MISSOURI FUR COMPANY in 1807.

Yellowstone River

Fort Cass

James River

Fort Pierre

Vermillion Post
Big Sioux Post
Ponca Post
Council Bluffs

Franklin

Fort HALL

SOUTH PASS over the Continental Divide

Fort Laramie
Fort St. Vrain

Platte River

Independence
Fort Osage

ST. LOUIS
Furs are shipped back East

Great SALT LAKE

Green River

River

Pikes Peak

SANTA FE TRAIL

Council Grove

OLD SPANISH TRAIL

Colorado River

BENT'S Fort

Cimarron CUTOFF

SANTA FE

Fort Dodge

Arkansas River

Canadian River

Precious little water for man or beast on this dangerous short cut.

GILA RIVER

To attract beavers, the trapper put "medicine" (castoreum: scent from a dead beaver's glands) on a willow switch set above a trap in a stream. When the animal's caught, it will drown.

Rio Grande

- ◨ Hudson's Bay Company trading post
- ◪ regional trading post
- ✺ Rendezvous sites
- ▲ major fur-trading depot

Narcissa

MARCUS

Men from the West come looking for the "book of heaven"

CHAPTER TWO

Narcissa, Marcus, and Dreams of Glory

MEDICINE QUEST

An eye-popping letter was printed on the front page of the March 1, 1833, edition of a Methodist newspaper. A fellow by the name of G. P. Disosway was passing on the story of an incredible journey.

In the summer of 1831, three men, H'co-a-h'co-a-h'cotes (Black Eagle), Hee-oh-'ks-te-kin (Rabbit Skin Leggings), and Tip-ya-lah-na-jah-nim (No Horns on His Head), traveled all the way from their Nez Perce territory in the Oregon Country to St. Louis, Missouri. With them was Ka-ou-pen (Man of the Morning), of

---

1813

May 22 —
Richard Wagner, *composer, is born in Germany.*

October 9 —
Guiseppe Verdi, *composer, is born in Italy.*

1813–1814 — *Creek War* —
Red Eagle *leads the fight for Creek Indian land in Mississippi Territory.* **Andrew Jackson's** *soldiers, including young* **Davy Crockett** *(see 1836), force the Creeks out at the 1814 Battle of Horseshoe Bend (Alabama).*

the Salish tribe, more commonly known as the Flatheads. They were on a quest.

To them, it seemed that light-skinned folks from back East had big medicine: more power and material goods than their people. And weren't folks' spiritual beliefs the basis for their strength in the world? That's how it was for the Indians. So they set off to see General William Clark, the Red-Headed Chief who'd come to visit them back in 1805 and 1806.

They hadn't understood each other very well back then, and, unfortunately, things hadn't changed much. The story of what the men wanted made it to the church folks back East by way of General Clark and a part-Wyandot man named William Walker, who relayed the Indians' message this way: "My people sent me to get the White Man's Book of Heaven..." There was even a picture of a cone-domed Flathead, which suggests that Walker lied or was confused. The Flatheads (a.k.a. Salish) did not deform the heads of their babies as did some other western tribes to whom the Salish's normal heads looked flat. The nickname might also have come from a gesture in the tribe's sign language.

Was it possible that there had been a bit of cultural mis-understanding? Perhaps so. It is certain that a powerful chain

1813

British government reigns in English nabobs (traders) of the East India Company, who've been getting rich off of India and her people for years.

Jane Austen writes Pride and Prejudice.

1814

George Stephenson invents an "iron horse," nickname for the first practical steam locomotive, a.k.a. "puffing billy."

of events, both bright and terrible, had been put in motion.

At least Man of the Morning never had to see his unflattering, pointy-headed picture in the *Christian Advocate*. He and Black Eagle got sick and died in St. Louis that fateful summer. Then, in 1832, No Horns on His Head and Rabbit Skin Leggings headed home on a steamboat. On the way, they got their portraits done by another passenger, a great painter of his time. George Catlin painted a pair of proudly feathered, handsome young men with long hair worn loose. Sad to say, but No Horns on his Head died of illness before he got home, and it wasn't long before Rabbit Skin Leggings was dead too, his scalp with its long black hair taken the hard way by a band of Blackfeet warriors.

George Catlin, historian with a paint brush

August 19–25 —
British troops raid Washington, DC. They burn the Capitol and the President's House. First Lady **Dolley Madison** *flees with important papers and* **George Washington's** *portrait.*

Thomas Jefferson *sells his collection of 6,400 books to the government to replace the destroyed Library of Congress.*

ARTIST-ADVENTURERS OF THE OLD WEST

In the centuries before cameras were invented, artists, were, among other things, eyewitness reporters. **Meriwether Lewis** did many fine, clear drawings of the plants and animals he saw on his 1804–06 expedition. When Stephen H. Long went exploring up the Platte River in 1819–20, he brought 20-year-old **Titian R. Peale**, one of a great family of artists, to record his observations.

Between 1826 and 1857, **George Catlin** traveled far to paint members of native tribes of North and South America. Curious Europeans and Americans came to see his educational exhibit, *Catlin's Indian Gallery*. In 1832–34, a Prussian prince went on a learning quest across the U.S., then up the Missouri River and back, along with **Karl Bodmer**, a 23-year-old Swiss painter who made hundreds of watercolor landscapes and portraits of Native Americans. Through the eyes and talent of **Alfred Jacob Miller**, we can glimpse the trappers' rendezvous and the Oregon Trail. Thanks to these artists and others who came after, such as William Henry Jackson, Alfred Bierstadt, Paul Kane, Frederic Remington, and Charles M. Russell, we can see what's gone forever: the Old West.

A few months later, the church folks back East were reading Mr. Disosway's letter in their paper: "Let the Church awake from her slumbers," he wrote, "and go forth in her strength to the salvation of those wandering sons of our native forests!"

Imagine the effect this had on all of those earnest people in the missionary societies! It wasn't long before a Methodist missionary, Jason Lee, was bound for the Oregon Country, which was claimed, by the way, by both the U S. and Great Britain.

A Presbyterian minister, Samuel Parker of Ithaca, New York, raised an alarm. Those Indians, those Wise Men from the West, were like the three kings in the Bible, looking for baby Jesus! Parker was determined to take the Presbyterian point of view to Oregon. But alas, when he arrived in St. Louis, it was almost June. Too late. Jason Lee and the fur company men, who were supposed to lead the way and offer protection, had already gone West for the season. The white-haired preacher went back East to raise money and get an early start for next year.

He bumped along in his wagon down rotten country roads between the towns of New York State, hunting for volunteers to go with him. He found 26-year-old Narcissa Prentiss and a restless country doctor.

1814

September 14 — Baltimore, MD — **Lawyer Francis Scott Key** *writes a poem after witnessing the British bombardment of Fort McHenry. The poem will be set to music and known as "The Star-Spangled Banner."*

Adieu, revolution. Bonjour, monarchy. **Napoleon** *is dead. Long live* **King Louis XVIII** *of France.*

South Africa — Dutch, a.k.a. Boers or Afrikaners, who'd been there since the 1650s, surrender the Cape Colony to the British (see 1836).

MARCUS

MARCUS WHITMAN'S LIFE BEGAN on September 4, 1802. Seven years later, his father died. Because poor Widow Whitman could not afford to care for all of her children, young Marcus was sent away from his mother and his brothers and sister to live with his grandfather and his uncle Freedom Whitman over in western Massachusetts. After graduating from a strict religious school, he wanted to study to be a minister, but that meant seven years of college. There wasn't any money for that. In his time, a person didn't need nearly so much book learning to be a lawyer or to heal folks, so Marcus chose medicine. And he went back to his hometown.

Marcus spent a few years apprenticing with Rushville's doctor, teaching school, getting reacquainted with his family, and helping out in their hide-tanning and shoe-making business. A 16-week course over at the school in Herkimer County got him

1815

January 8 —
No phones so nobody in America knew that peace papers had been signed in Belgium. So two weeks after the War of 1812 was over, its last battle was fought when **Andrew Jackson** *walloped the British at the Battle of New Orleans and became a national hero.*

June 9 —
After **Napoleon's** *wars, Europe is in tatters. Now its map is redrawn at the Congress of Vienna.*

a license to practice medicine. A few more months of study later on earned him a medical degree. Young Dr. Whitman rode his horse around Canada, Pennsylvania, and New York, giving out pills, stitching up some patients, and "bleeding" others, letting out the bad blood. He probably wished, in this pre-anesthesia time, that he had something better in his black bag than *laudanum* (made from opium) or whiskey to stop people's pain.

He went to church every time its doors opened and studied theology books in his spare time, still wishing he might be a preacher someday. All in all, it was a pretty unsatisfied guy who looked up to see visiting Reverend Samuel Parker stand up behind the pulpit in November 1834. Who, the old man asked, would come with him into the West?

Young Doc Whitman, letting out the bad blood

June 18 – Belgium –
The deadly Napoleonic wars grind to an end. British **General Wellington**, *"the Iron Duke," and his forces defeat the French at the Battle of Waterloo and end* **Napoleon Bonaparte's** *quest to rule all of Europe.*

June 17–30 — Mediterranean Sea, African coast —
For years, Barbary pirates have raided ships and demanded tribute (bribes) from anyone near their ports in Algiers, Tunis, and Tripoli.

Narcissa Prentiss, Preacher Parker, and Marcus Whitman

1815

Now **Commodore Stephen Decatur** settles the pirates' hash once and for all and America gets a great naval hero.

Fewer coal mines blow up, thanks to **Humphry Davy's** invention: the coal miner's safety lamp.

November 12 — **Elizabeth Cady Stanton**, suffragist (right-to-vote activist), is born in New York.

HELLO, GOOD-BYE

JUST A FEW MILES OF FARM COUNTRY and bad roads separated their towns, so it's possible that Narcissa Prentiss and Marcus Whitman had met each other at church. Perhaps he'd heard her sing and admired her clear soprano voice. Maybe she'd seen his blue eyes and noticed his dark hair with its peculiar strands of white. In any event, Samuel Parker had met them both. He knew that Narcissa, missionary-volunteer, was looking for a husband. And if Marcus was going to doctor the Indians, a missionary wife would come in handy.

Narcissa's family had moved to the village of Amity, New York. Marcus showed up there on Saturday, February 21, 1835. By Sunday, he and Narcissa were engaged. They'd get married as soon as he got back from the West. The church officials weren't ready to risk sending a delicate lady out on an unheard of journey

An 1815 volcano in the East Indies is partly to blame for June snows in North America, this summerless year of "eighteen and froze to death."

Germany —
Baron Karl von Drais *invents the draisine, a kind of walk-along bicycle (see 1839).*

France —
Dr. Rene Laennec *is working on a new invention: a stethoscope.*

into the frontier until Dr. Whitman and Reverend Parker checked it out.

Narcissa waved good-bye to her new fiancé. Marcus turned his horse westward. What they all were thinking, one can only imagine.

In St. Louis, Missouri, April 8, 1835, Marcus and Parker were listening to bells clanging and squinting up at the lofty pilot house of their steamboat. Black smoke poured out of its chimneys, up from the furnaces. They heated the water in the boilers so steam could push the paddlewheels, churning against the hard-driving spring current of light-catching liquid mud known as the Missouri River. If all went well, if an uprooted tree didn't stab the boat in its guts or the boilers didn't blow them all to heavenly glory, they could expect to be in Liberty, Missouri, 250 miles away, in about a week. That's where the travelers would buy their animals and supplies.

Marcus and Parker met up with a Baptist preacher planning on converting the Oto Indians up on the Platte River (Nebraska, these days). The trio of missionaries hooked up with Lucien Fontenelle, who was leading 200 mules and horses, 3 teams of oxen, 6 wagons, and 60 pretty rough characters. This caravan was

1816

Argentina declares independence from Spain. **General José de San Martin** leads the fight.

Spanish-held Florida — **General Andrew Jackson** fights the Spanish and the local Indians in the First Seminole War.

April 21 — **Charlotte Brontë**, author, is born in England.

December 11 — Indiana becomes 19th state in the Union.

bringing whiskey, money, supplies, and trade goods to a Rocky Mountain meadow where hundreds of fur trappers were waiting to swap a year's worth of "peltry at the annual rendezvous."

Marcus found that he'd signed up for Frontier Travel 101. He learned: (1) Packing a mule so all of one's supplies didn't fall off as soon as the mule started walking was not easy. (2) Neither was raft- and bridge-building so you could get across swollen creeks or (3) building a fire with wet wood or no wood at all. (4) Marcus and his fellow travelers got on each other's nerves. Samuel Parker, a good man, was also a 56-year-old fusspot of a boss. The teamsters cussed and threw rotten eggs at the church-men when they refused to take a drink or travel on Sundays. Only when Dr. Whitman saved Fontenelle and most of the men from cholera, a horrible, deadly disease, did they begin to treat him kindly.

At the rendezvous, Marcus met legendary Westerners Christopher "Kit" Carson and Joe Lafayette Meek and loads of folks who hadn't had any proper doctoring in a long while, if ever. He earned some good will from Jim Bridger, the first white man to see the Great Salt Lake. Marcus dug an arrowhead out of its three-year resting place in the frontiersman's aching back.

1817

British government pays **Lord Elgin** $159,600 *for the marble sculptures he'd taken away from Athens' ancient Acropolis with the permission of Greece's Turkish rulers.*

Sir David Brewster *patents his new invention: the kaleidoscope.*

French pirate **Jean Laffite**, *who helped* **Andrew Jackson** *win the Battle of New Orleans, establishes a pirate colony and a fine smuggling operation on Galveston Island, off the coast of Texas.*

muskrat: 25¢ elk: $1 opossum: 10¢

What do you get for an animal's skin? 1835.

MOUNTAIN MAN RENDEZVOUS

William Ashley and his partner jump-started the Rocky Mountain fur trade with their 1822 want-ad for enterprising young trappers. They'd provide equipment, get them up the Missouri River to the "beaver country," then split the profits from the furs. Instead of financing isolated trading posts, the traders hit on the idea of meeting up with the trappers. Ashley put out the word in 1824. Amazingly, at the end of June 1825, more than a hundred trappers came out of the wilderness to a mountain valley south of the present-day Utah-Wyoming border. Ashley, his men, and pack mules had come 1,200 miles to meet them. They brought money, supplies, and trade goods for bartering and swapping: buttons, mirrors, combs, blankets, scissors, beads, *vermillion*

25¢ each. coyote: 50¢ wolf: 74¢

beaver : $6 per pound   otter : $4 per pound

deer : 27¢

buffalo : $2.50

wild cat, badger, fox, or raccoon :

(red pigment for paint), pipes, and twists of tobacco. In return for such things, supplies, and money, the traders reaped a fur bonanza. This frontier payday/trade fair, combined with whiskey and rough men reuniting with old friends, added up to a rowdy time known as the mountain man rendezvous (RAHN-day-voo).

Whooping, singing, dancing; shooting matches, fistfights and fiddle playing; gambling; and stories and jokes told around hundreds of campfires. People carried on for a week or more. Until 1840, when the fur trade would pretty much give out, thousands of frontier folk, their families, dogs, and horses got together every summer.

Doc Whitman and preacher Parker came to some bold decisions at the rendezvous. When the traders took the year's fur harvest back to St. Louis, impatient Marcus would go with them. He'd hurry on East, collect his bride, and together they'd return to Oregon in 1836, a full year earlier than originally planned. Meanwhile, Parker would go on West with the Indians and check out the best place for the mission. With their fathers' blessings, it was decided that two Nez Perce boys, Tackitonitis and Ais — soon to be known as Richard and John — would go with Marcus to New York State. When they returned next summer, they

Strange new world: Nez Perce boys in town

1817

February 12 —
Chile wins free-
dom from Spain
in the Battle of
Chacabuco.

March 4 —
James Monroe
is 5th President.

July 4 — Rome, NY —
Digging begins on the
Erie Canal.

Reverend Richard Allen,
former slave, founds the
African Methodist Episcopal
(A.M.E.) Church.

would have a better knowledge of each other's languages and ways.

It took over three months for the travelers to get from Wyoming to western New York. Imagine two Indian boys, their wide eyes full of stagecoaches, steamboats, clustered buildings with glass windows, and pale, curious faces rimmed with beards or bonnets. Their ears were filled with strange talk, bells, and factory whistles. It was December when Marcus Whitman surprised his family, and Narcissa's waiting and wondering was cut short by the sight of him in her snowy doorway.

Marcus and Narcissa didn't have much time. In order to be

A surprise visitor

1818

July 12 —
Henry David Thoreau, *author, is born in Massachusetts.*

December 10 —
The Union gets its 20th state: Mississippi.

Dr. James Parkinson *describes and defines a nervous disorder: Parkinson's Disease.*

Jons Jakob Berzelius, *who came up with modern chemical symbols, publishes the molecular weights of 2,000 chemical compounds.*

in the Oregon Country by fall, before mountain snows blocked their way, they had to be at the trappers' rendezvous by summer and by spring, at the far edge of Missouri to meet the fur traders' caravan. But none of this would happen if they didn't talk another couple into going with them. It wouldn't be safe or proper for Narcissa to be the only woman on this rugged adventure. That's why, one winter day, Marcus Whitman was out in his sleigh, calling to Henry and Eliza Spalding, "We want you for Oregon!"

THE SPALDINGS

THIN, DARK-HAIRED ELIZA was 28 years old, four years younger than her husband, a grim soul ever since his unwed mother abandoned him when he was little. It hadn't helped Henry Spalding's attitude any, having pretty Narcissa Prentiss turn him down when he had asked her to marry him. All for the best,

1818

April 4 —
The Congress decides that the U.S. flag will have 13 stripes and a new star for each new state.

May 5 —
Karl Marx, philosopher, revolutionary, is born in Germany.

May 27 —
Amelia Jenks Bloomer, reformer, is born in New York. Her "Turkish pantaloons" will make her infamous.

July 30 —
Emily Brontë, author, is born in England.

actually. He ended up with Eliza Hart, and a fine team they were.

Like all female teachers then, Eliza Hart Spalding had to give up her job when she got married — not exactly fair, but that's how it was. Henry worked his way through college out in Ohio, chopping wood, working in a print shop, and helping Eliza run a boarding house. Side by side, they studied Latin, Greek, and Hebrew. Eliza had a knack for drawing, too. Someday, Eliza would outdo all of the others at communicating with her new Indian neighbors.

A very religious pair the Spaldings were, with lots of friends devoted to passionate, serious talk. In their world were the great Beecher preachers: Lyman and Henry Ward, father and son; big sisters, Catharine, the educator, and Harriet, world-famous author of *Uncle Tom's Cabin*. Even more world-changing were books by their friend William McGuffey. He was working on America's very first illustrated books designed to teach kids how to read. More than 120 million people would buy copies of *McGuffey's Eclectic Reader*. It's a cinch that he gave Eliza and Henry definite ideas — maybe even sent books — about reaching their own future students when at last, after many difficulties, their dream of becoming missionaries would come true.

Mary Wollstonecraft Shelley *writes* Frankenstein.

December 3 — *Illinois becomes the Union's 21st state.*

Joseph Mohr: Stille Nacht, Heilige Nacht, *"Silent Night"* (*tune by* **Franz Xavier Gruber**)

South Africa — **Shaka**, *great Zulu king, as much of a military genius as his better known European counterparts,* **Napoleon** *and* **Wellington**, *begins racking up victories, empire building.*

Henry and Eliza Spalding were all set to go to work with the Osage Indians in an established mission no farther west than Oklahoma. Now they were being asked to tackle a next-to-impossible trip to the back end of beyond? When Eliza was still weak from giving birth to a stillborn baby? With Narcissa? The woman who had spurned Henry before Eliza came along?

In the end, Eliza decided that their Christian duty was to the poor native souls in Oregon.

They'd go.

It meant facing hundreds and hundreds of miles of hard traveling away from everything familiar. It was a phoneless world in which a letter from home could take two years to get to you. To most Easterners, it meant going through horrid difficulties to get someplace almost unimaginably foreign and faraway from which one might never return. Ah well, Narcissa, Marcus, Eliza, and Henry were made of stern stuff. They were eager to tackle their noble adventure.

So candles blazed in the Presbyterian Church of Angelica, New York. Narcissa Prentiss put on her new black dress and married Dr. Marcus Whitman on February 18, 1836. Wiping their eyes, the congregation sang a missionary hymn. Only Narcissa's

1819

Fabian von Bellingshausen, *a Russian explorer, and* Nathaniel B. Palmer, *an American seal hunter, glimpse an undiscovered continent: Antarctica (see 1840).*

New York — Jethro Wood *invents an improved cast-iron plow.*

Bad economic times in the U.S. and a big angry question: Will Missouri, with its slave owners, become a state? In the Congress, Henry Clay *will find a "Missouri Compromise" (1820). Maine's entry in the Union would keep the balance of slave and free states, 12 each. To* Thomas Jefferson, *an old ex-president, the political ruckus was "a fire-bell in the night."*

voice was steady enough to sing the last lines: "Let me hasten, let me hasten/ Far in heathen lands to dwell." Young Richard/ Tackitonitis left town the next day with the bride and groom. Never on this Earth did hard-weeping Narcissa, her mother and father, brothers and sisters, see each other again.

Hard to say "good-bye"

May 8 —
Death of wise king
Kamehameha I
of Hawaii

May 22–June 20 —
First voyage (Savannah, Georgia to Liverpool, England) of steam-powered vessel, the U.S.S. Savannah

May 24 —
Princess Alexandrina Victoria is born in London (see 1838).

The missionaries head out across the rolling prairie.

CHAPTER THREE

The Journey

FEBRUARY 19 – MAY 3

Angelica, New York, to Liberty, Missouri

BEFORE GOING WEST, THE WHITMANS headed east to Ithaca to collect John/Ais, who was staying with Samuel Parker's family, then to Rushville, where Marcus's big brother, Augustus, made some sturdy boots for his new sister-in-law. Church folks there passed the collection plate for the newlywed pioneers. They wanted to hear Marcus preach and get a good look at the bride who was going where none of them had ever gone and who was going to have the-good-Lord-Himself-only-knew-what-sort-of adventures.

1819

May 27 —
Julia Ward Howe is born in New York. This public speaker, reformer, and poet wrote "Battle Hymn of the Republic" (1861) and came up with this idea: Mother's Day.

May 31 —
Walt Whitman, poet (no relation to Marcus), is born in New York.

December 14 —
The Union gets its 22nd state: Alabama.

December 16 —
By **Ludwig van Beethoven**'s 49th birthday, he is totally deaf. Only in his mind can he hear his music.

Farewell, farewell, and away they went, on March 3, 1836, off to Pittsburgh, Pennsylvania. Aboard the steamboat *Siam*, they'd go down the Ohio River to meet the Spaldings in Cincinnati. They, too, had come by way of Pittsburgh, where they struck up a conversation with George Catlin, the frontier artist who'd painted Rabbit Skin Leggings. When he found out where Henry and Eliza were going, the painter was appalled. Delicate ladies? Riding sidesaddle? In buffalo country? Around all sorts of people? In dust and rain storms, under the hot sun and the open sky? Outrageous! Dangerous!

Did this make Eliza want to turn back? Oh, no. Frail she was, but steely, too.

On their journey, Narcissa, Marcus, Eliza, and Henry met other church folks intending to live among the Indians but not nearly so far West. When they got to St. Louis, newspaperman Elijah Lovejoy sought them out. Unlike his abolitionist editorials, a nice story about missionary ladies on a breakthrough journey wouldn't make his pro-slavery readers so mad. Next year, he'd move across the Mississippi to Illinois, hoping to be safer in a "free" state (*see the Time Line: 1837*).

While they were in the bustling town, the missionaries

1819   **1820**

Geoffrey Crayon, *a.k.a.* **Washington Irving,** *writes* The Sketch Book, *including* "The Legend of Sleepy Hollow" *and* "Rip van Winkle."

U.S. population: 9,638,453. 1,771,656 are black; 90% of these are enslaved.

Protestant missionaries begin arriving in the Hawaiian Islands.

Maryland —
It's possible that **Araminta Ross,** *better known later on as* **Harriet Tubman** *or even "Moses," was born this year. Records are uncertain for babies born into slavery.*

checked out St. Louis's new cathedral, and culture-shocked Narcissa saw a way of worship entirely new to her. She heard music "very different from our church tunes" and didn't much care for such Catholic "splendor and show."

Married life was pretty unfamiliar to her, too, but judging from her lively letters to her sister, Narcissa was sure she liked Marcus. "Jane, if you want to be happy get as good a husband as I have got, and be a missionary." Here's how the bride described a spring evening on the river.

"Twilight had nearly gone when we entered the waters of the great Missouri, but the moon shone in her brightness....My husband and myself went upon the top of the boat, to take a more commanding view of the scenery...how grand was the scene! the meeting of two such great waters...I could have dwelt upon the scene still longer with pleasure, but Brother Spalding called us to prayers...."

Three more steamboats, the *Junius*, the *Majestic*, and the *Chariton*, got them to Liberty, Missouri, on April 7, where Marcus had had his first lesson in loading a pack mule only a year before. Some of the *Chariton* passengers might well have traveled on to Independence, at the eastern end of the Santa Fe Trail. Later on, that

John Keats' *poem,* Ode on a Grecian Urn, *includes this line: "Beauty is truth, truth beauty..."*

A discovery on the Greek isle of Melos: the beautiful but armless **Venus de Milo**. *The goddess had her arms in the 2nd century B.C. when she was carved and sculpted.*

Walter Scott *writes* Ivanhoe.

town would become the best known place to leave the States and head out for Oregon or California, but it wasn't the only one. Along the bend of the Missouri River were several good "jumping off" towns, such as Westport (now part of present-day Kansas City), Weston, and St. Joseph (all in Missouri), as well as Fort Leavenworth, or Nebraska City. Some rode the steamers as far north as Council Bluffs, where the Platte River meets the Missouri.

On April 19, another steamboat stopped at the Liberty landing, and William Henry Gray walked down the gangplank. He was a carpenter with missionary ambitions of his own, sent by the Mission Board to travel with the Spaldings, Whitmans, and the Nez Perce boys.

The plan was that the steamboat *Diana* would stop on her way up the Missouri River and pick up Marcus, Narcissa, and Eliza. Meanwhile, Henry, the boys, and Mr. Gray would take their supplies and animals overland to where they'd meet up with the American Fur Company caravan, led this year by the tough Irish mountain man Tom "Broken Hand" Fitzpatrick. The fur traders would guide and protect the missionaries on their trip to the Oregon Country. It was all arranged.

For the journey, Eliza Spalding's father had given her and

1820

January 29 — England —
King George III
is dead at 81.

February 15 —
Susan B. Anthony,
suffragist, is born in New York.

March 15 —
A year after it splits off from Massachusetts, Maine becomes the 23rd state.

May 12 —
Florence Nightingale,
nurse, reformer, is born in Italy.

Henry a light, one-horse "Dearborn" wagon, painted blue and yellow. Marcus bought a big farm wagon, too, to carry all their supplies for their new lives at the mission. In 1836, no one had gotten anything with wheels all the way to Oregon, but Marcus, who hadn't yet been over the mountains, was sure that he could get the job done. This would be an important breakthrough. Restless families in the East would be eager to know: Could they load up their own farm wagons and go into the mysterious West?

While Narcissa and Eliza were sewing their striped, tepee-shaped tent for the trip, Marcus, Henry, the Indian boys, then Mr. Gray, went tramping about muddy Liberty, stopping in at all of the outfitters, stores, and livery stables, spending $3,063.96 (more than $50,000 in today's money) on what all they'd need: A dozen horses, $118.00 worth of cattle — 17 (4 of them milk cows, while the others could be meat along the way) — and 6 mules (they and the horses cost $926.00); garden seeds, medicines, tools, tin plates, cups, knives and forks, and guns and ammunition, although Marcus and Henry didn't like the idea of using them. They also bought harness and saddles, including a pair of side-saddles for their wives.

July 14–15 — Colorado — *Men of the* **Stephen Long** *Expedition climb* *[Zebulon] Pike's Peak.*

September 26 — *Trailblazer* **Daniel Boone** *dies at age 85,* *in Missouri.*

Boston — **William Underwood** *opens America's first food canning plant.*

In earlier times, genteel customs only allowed a lady to sit behind her horse-riding gentleman — not straddling the animal, but on a cushion-like pillion as if the horse were a tall, moving couch. But Eliza and Narcissa were modern women. They rode sidesaddle: Left foot in its stirrup, right leg hooked around sort of a peg. Sitting sideways like that made for a fine backache, and a rider was more apt to fall off her horse, but until then she at least had the satisfaction of knowing that she looked like a proper, elegant lady.

Narcissa and Eliza riding sidesaddle, as proper ladies should

"Mrs. Spalding does not look or feel quite healthy enough for our enterprise. Riding affects her differently from what it does me," Narcissa bragged. "Everyone who sees me compliments me as being the best able to endure the journey over the mountains....I like [Mrs. Spalding] very much," and Mrs.

1821

February 3 — **Elizabeth Blackwell**, *first woman in the U.S. to receive a medical degree, is born in England.*

William Becknell *opens the 780-mile-long Santa Fe Trail.*

Sequoya *perfects his alphabet and system for writing the Cherokee language.*

Whitman added, "She is a very suitable person for Mr. Spalding."

Mr. Spalding, Mr. Gray, young Richard and John, and a hired hand, plus the livestock and loaded wagons rattled and clip-clopped out of Liberty, Missouri, on April 27.

All this time, you should know, the missionaries had also been helping Dr. Satterlee, one of their fellow travelers, take care of his frail young wife. Sicker and sicker she got until she died at the end of April. Just as Marcus and the others were getting her properly buried, they saw the smoke. They heard the bells. A steamboat was coming up the river!

They waved and shouted at the *Diana*. Her captain, who'd missed the memo about picking anybody up at Liberty, waved and shouted back across the water that he was already too crowded, and he wouldn't stop. As Marcus, Narcissa, and Eliza watched, *Diana*'s paddle wheels carried the captain and his passengers around the bend in the river. They were stranded.

And if they couldn't catch up with Henry and their baggage and the fur company caravan — well, that didn't bear thinking about. Marcus scrambled to hire a team and wagon and on the 3rd of May, he and the ladies clattered across the hills.

It was going to be a bumpy ride.

The Ottomans, based in Turkey, started grabbing Greece in the 1300s. Now Greeks begin a fierce, cruel war for independence from the Turks (see 1829).

Mexico breaks away from Spanish rule. Texas and California are part of the new Mexican empire.

Spain loses control of Florida (see 1822).

PREPARING FOR THE JOURNEY

You're going West: a HUGE decision. Now you have more critical choices to make. When do you leave? From which Missouri River town? And how will you move everything? (As for your wagon and how to make it go, see page 69.) Besides rope, tools, tin plates, cooking pots, clothes, candles, keepsakes, bedding, and sturdy walking shoes, what do you pack?

Many pioneers load a medicine box with herbs, whiskey, and such things as pain-killing laudanum, castor oil for digestion troubles, clove oil for toothache, quinine for malaria, camphor for cholera, and citric acid for scurvy after you've eaten all the fruits and vegetables you packed.

You've got to carry supplies for a trip which, if all goes well, takes four to six months. In his 1847 guidebook, *Journal of Travels Over the Rocky Mountains*, Joel Palmer recommended at least 200 pounds of flour, 30 pounds of hardtack, 75 pounds of bacon (pack it in bran, to keep it fresh a little longer), 10 pounds of rice, 25 pounds of sugar in "India rubber" bags to keep it dry, 5 pounds of coffee, 2 pounds of tea, half a bushel each of cornmeal and dried beans (pack eggs and china in these so they won't break), a bushel of dried fruit, 2 pounds of *saleratus* (baking soda), and 10 pounds of salt **for each adult**. And think twice about packing Pa's oak desk. It could wind up being a roadside attraction.

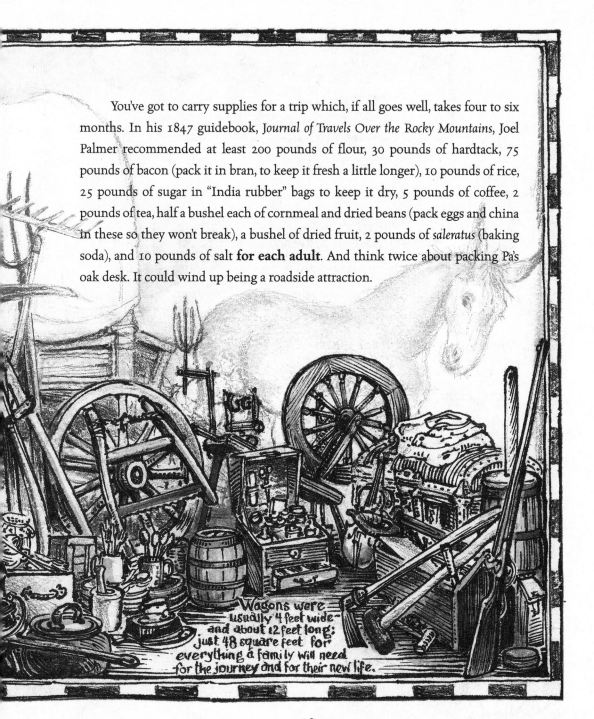

Wagons were usually 4 feet wide and about 12 feet long: just 48 square feet for everything a family will need for the journey and for their new life.

MAY 3 – MAY 26
Liberty, Missouri, to the Catch Up (Nebraska)

TO US HERE IN THE FUTURE, accustomed to fast cars, asphalt, and road maps, a road trip by horse-drawn wagon over bumpy, rolling ground is a slow-going deal. Getting from one side of a simple stream, down and up its steep, muddy banks, was a tough proposition. Thirty miles from Liberty, half an hour on the freeway these days, was Fort Leavenworth, where the missionaries hoped to find Henry Spalding's tiny caravan. They got ferried over the Missouri River, which wouldn't be bridged for another 30 years. They rode for two days, slept at night with only blankets between them and the earth and stars, and finally got to the fort, but was Henry there? No.

They didn't find each other until the middle of May. Separated again, lost, reunited again, slowed by sickness, a wagon

1821

El Libertador (*The Liberator*) **Simon Bolivar**, the "*George Washington of South America*," *is warrior/leader of independence movement. Venezuela, Columbia, Peru, Bolivia, Panama, and Ecuador throw off Spanish control.*

Stephen Austin *of Missouri brings 300 families to Mexican Texas: the beginning of an American colony (see 1835).*

breakdown — all this before they had to cross three rivers. In this time before bridges, each fast-moving river, high and fat with melted snow and spring rains, made a pretty substantial barrier.

At the Platte, Marcus, Richard, and John took off their shirts and wound them tightly around their heads. They tied rope to a canoe, then swam alongside load after load of heavy baggage until everything and everybody were on the desired bank of the river. It took two whole days. A hard-to-navigate boat made of buffalo skins helped them across the Elkhorn. After another ride and a lot more hard effort, they and their load and livestock made it across one of the forks of the Loup River.

All one Sunday they were on the move, a desperate decision by folks who believed that God expected them to sit tight and rest on the Sabbath. Another long, plodding day, they drove themselves across 60 miles of prairie. "It is astonishing," Narcissa wrote later on, "how well we get along with our wagons where there are no roads." At last, in the first black hour of the 26th of May, the exhausted people and animals saw golden flickers: campfires.

Wagons were silhouetted against the dark sky and pale tents. The spring night was filled with the restless sounds made by hundreds of mules and horses. Captain Fitzpatrick's caravan!

May 5 — St. Helena — *Ex-emperor, military genius, conqueror, dictator,* **Napoleon Bonaparte** *dies at his island prison.*

June 1 — Troy, NY — **Emma Hart Willard** *opens women's first institution for higher education.*

July 16 — **Mary Baker Eddy,** *founder of Christian Science, is born in New Hampshire.*

The two Eastern ladies had had a brisk initiation into frontier travel. Marcus Whitman wrote, "We thanked God and took courage." As for his bride, writing about their honeymoon: "Was there ever a journey like this?"

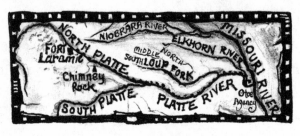

MAY 26 – JUNE 13
Across Nebraska along the Platte River Road,
up to Fort Laramie (Wyoming)

ALTOGETHER THERE WERE "NEARLY 400 ANIMALS, with ours," Narcissa wrote, "mostly mules, and 70 men...we cover quite a space." Far up at the front of their moving village was Captain Tom "Broken Hand" Fitzpatrick and his buddy from their fur-trapping days, Moses "Black" Harris, also known as the Black Squire. A nobleman from Scotland accompanied the caravan, too. Sir William Drummond Stewart was loaded with money

1821   **1822**

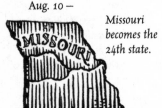

Aug. 10 —
Missouri becomes the 24th state.

December 25 —
Clara Barton, battlefield nurse, founder of American Red Cross, is born in Massachusetts.

South Carolina —
Former slave
Denmark Vesey
and about 35 followers are hanged after their planned slave rebellion fails.

Yellow fever kills almost 400 people in New York City.

and generally had a high old time on his annual holiday in the wild American West. Next year, he'd bring along a suit of armor, a fine present for Jim Bridger.

Riding in a cart was Milton, one of the Sublette brothers, a big man who was still recovering from having his leg cut off (remember: no anesthesia yet). Apaches had wounded him when he was fur-trapping in their southwestern lands. One-legged Milton Sublette's future adventures would earn him a cool nickname: Thunderbolt of the Rocky Mountains.

Going West with the caravan

Florida becomes an official U.S. Territory (see 1845).

West Africa — The Ashanti and the Fanti people war with each other for the rest of the decade.

Africa — Members of the American Colonization Society start Monrovia, a settlement in a land to be known as Liberia, populated with freed slaves from America (see 1847).

Loaded pack mules went in single file, then the fur company's seven wagons, each drawn by six mules, then the Whitmans and Spaldings in one wagon and on horseback, Mr. Gray and the baggage in another, then the cattle, and finally John and Richard, the Nez Perce cowboys, riding alongside.

They were following a natural road across the high prairie, along the valley of the wide, shallow Platte River. Later on, writers would say that the Oregon Trail was like a rope, raveled at each end. In the East, there were almost as many ways to get from the States to the Platte as there were travelers. In the West, where the land was rougher, there'd be shortcuts and wanderings to different destinations, but in between was the Platte River valley. Native travelers, wagons full of *emigrants* (folks on their way to live someplace else), Mormons, trouble-driven out of Missouri and Illinois, going to the Great Salt Lake, the Gold Rushers of 1849, Pony Express riders in 1860–61, modern drivers on Interstate 80 — they all go the way of the Platte.

Narcissa was having the happy time of her life. At daybreak, men called out, "Arise! Arise!" adding their voices to those of the prairie birds: cowbirds, kestrels, sparrows, and larks. "Then," Narcissa

1822

January 6 —
Heinrich Schliemann,
*archeologist who'll discover
the ruins of ancient Troy,
is born in Germany.*

*Ottoman Turks kill tens
of thousands of rebellious
Greeks on island of Chios.*

April 27 —
Ulysses S. Grant,
*soldier, president, is
born in Ohio.*

wrote, "the mules set up such a noise as you never heard, which puts the whole camp in motion....While the horses are feeding we get breakfast in a hurry and eat it. By this time the words,

Dropping by to say "hello"

'Catch up! Catch up', ring through the camp for moving. We are ready to start usually at six, travel till eleven, encamp, rest and feed, and start again about two." They'd travel another four hours until they camped for the night, having covered, on average, 20 miles.

One evening early on, the Pawnees, who lived in villages nearby, came to visit. They peeped into the striped tent and beamed astonished grins at the two women.

July 22 —
Gregor Mendel, *botanist, founder of science of genetics, is born in Austria (Czech Republic, now).*

December 27 —
Louis Pasteur, *scientist, is born in France.*

Pianist **Franz Liszt**, *11 years old, makes his debut in Vienna. In the 1830s, he'll be rock-star famous all over Europe.*

"We ladies were such a curiosity to them," Narcissa wrote in a letter home. She was impressed, too, with the "noble" Pawnees, their "large athletic forms" and dignified faces, "bespeaking an immortal existence within."

The Pawnee lived in the land of the buffalo, more properly called bison. In Narcissa's time, North America's herd numbered about 20 million. The prairie could appear to be a black, moving

Bygone bison days

1823

Scientist **Michael Faraday**, *who's already liquefied gases, puts them under pressure until they condense and chill — a big step toward mechanical refrigerators (see 1834).*

England — Game of rugby is invented.

October 9 — **Mary Ann Shadd Cary**, *abolitionist, African-American educator, journalist, is born in Delaware.*

sea of buffalo. To a traveler in 1846, they sounded "like an approaching earthquake." By 1889, after years of hunting madness, less than 600 American bison would still be alive. In parklands, farms, and game preserves, there are about 300,000 now.

Narcissa saw her first buffalo near present-day North Platte, Nebraska. She and Eliza Spalding jumped out of the wagon in which they often rode, rather than ride horseback. They "ran upon the bluff," all the better to see the shaggy-coated buffalo bull who'd crossed their path. Just think: A full-grown bull can weigh anywhere from 1,600 to 3,000 pounds and measure 10 to 12 feet from nose to tufted tail! And the missionary ladies weren't the only ones chasing buffalo. Captain Fitzpatrick's men killed several of them that day, cut out their tongues (a great delicacy), carved out the ribs from the animals' humps, and left the rest to rot. That's what white hunters generally did, unlike Native Americans, who used all they could of the precious beast for clothing, weapons, food, and shelter. And fuel: "prairie coal." *Bois de vache,* French for "wood from the cow," a.k.a. buffalo chips. Non-stinky, dried bison poop fueled fine campfires.

Buffalo would be what's-for-dinner that night and for many thereafter. Narcissa, it turned out, had married a man who'd learned

1824

New opera this year, Clari or the Maid of Milan *has a huge hit song:* "Home Sweet Home" *by* **John Howard Payne** (words) *and* **Henry R. Bishop** (tune).

*December 23 —
A new poem is printed in the* Troy (NY) Sentinel: "An Account of a Visit from St. Nicholas" a.k.a. "The Night Before Christmas." **Clement Clarke Moore** — *or* **Henry Livingston** — *wrote it.*

Russia agrees to let some of its Alaskan territory go to the U.S. and Great Britain.

more than one way to cook it. This was handy since there were many trail days when it was all there was to eat. "So long as I have buffalo meat I do not wish anything else," wrote cheerful Narcissa, and that their meat and tea diet had made poor "Sister Spalding" sick.

Fitzpatrick's caravan passed O'Fallon's Bluff, a landmark he knew well from his earlier trips; then the forks, where the Platte River split. Tom Fitzpatrick took the north fork. As the mules, horses, people, and cattle toiled westward, up, over, and down the prairie swells, theirs was basically an uphill trek towards the Rocky Mountains. Still, they faced some dangerous downhill struggles such as the scary descent down Windlass Hill. Travelers would write about setting their brakes, using ropes and chains, sometimes tying whole trees to their wagons to keep them from careening downhill too fast, crashing and crushing their animals to death.

As the terrain grew rougher, Marcus, Henry, and the mules were having a terrible time getting their heavy wagon over the land. For pioneer travelers, wagon breakdowns were as much a fact of life as prairie winds and head-banging hailstorms. They carried spare hardwood axles if they could, greased their hubs

1824

The Marquis de Lafayette, *old hero of the American Revolution, survivor of the French Revolution, makes a grand return visit and tours the U.S.*

Burma goes to war, trying to avoid becoming part of the British Empire.

Ludwig van Beethoven *composes his 9th Symphony (Choral).*

and soaked their wheels in water, and still the dry western air cracked wooden spokes out of the wooden wheels, which shrank away from the iron rims.

Marcus considered lightening the load by ditching his extra clothes, but all that got him was his first argument with Narcissa. In the next decades, the Oregon Trail would be littered with discarded spinning wheels, books, pump organs, and iron stoves. Folks learned to make do with a covered kettle and a *spider* (a frying pan with legs to keep it up out of the fire) for cooking on the trail. Feet tramped and wheels rolled past the bones and decaying carcasses of worn-out oxen whose bleached skulls made a fine note pad on which you could scrawl a message for whomever might be coming down the trail. Humans died along the way, too, far and away more often because of sickness or injury than because of Indian attacks. Graves were carefully marked or, more likely, disguised by rolling over the mound with the wagon. Folks feared their loved ones being dug up by wolves or two-legged grave robbers.

About a day's journey beyond Ash Hollow, named for the grove of ash trees there, overlanders glimpsed mighty rock formations.

April 19 — Greece — **George Gordon,** *a.k.a.* **Lord Byron,** *famous, colorful, poet/heartthrob, dies when he goes to fight for Greek independence from the Turks.*

September 30 — **Jim Bridger** *discovers* **Great Salt Lake.**

December 1 — Presidential candidates **Andrew Jackson, John Quincy Adams, William H. Crawford,** *and* **Henry Clay** *have run such a tight race that it will have to be decided next year in the Congress.*

Cotton or linen **cover**, waterproofed with linseed oil, is stretched over **bows made** of HICKORY wood.

brake lever

pocket

jockey box holds tools.

hub (ELM or OSAGE ORANGE)

axle and tire (IRON)

wagon tongue (HICKORY)

spoke (OAK) felloe (ASH)

To keep them turning smoothly, the hubs and wheels are greased with tar and tallow (animal fat).

THE GREAT WAGON DEBATE

By the time you step off the steamboat at Independence or Westport, Missouri, you'll have heard lots of arguments over which animals make the best wagon-pulling "engine." Horses are fastest, but you have to pack extra feed. Tough, surefooted mules (horse + donkey = mule) can live on grass and just about anything growing along the trail. Most folks used slow, patient oxen, which cost half as much, from $30 to $60 per pair, and didn't need complicated harnesses — just a wooden yoke. One pioneer wrote that the ox "was the noblest of draft animals on that trip, and possessed more hardihood and pluck than either mules or horses." As for your wagon, it must be light but strong enough to carry perhaps a ton of baggage over 2,000 miles of hard country.

yoke

Their names came from what they looked like to some folks: the Courthouse and the Jail. Like awesome, storm-carved castles, they were 400 feet tall, made of sandstone, volcanic ash, and clay. Beyond them was the trail's most famous landmark, a cone-shaped mound topped with what looked like a chimney.

Four years earlier, Benjamin Bonneville, a French explorer and fur trader, wrote about it "rising out of the naked plain; from the summit shoots up a shaft or column...seen at the distance of upwards of thirty miles." As travelers neared Chimney Rock, it grew and grew until there it was: a marvelous sight like nothing they'd ever seen. It stands 325 feet tall, shorter than it used to be, thanks to wind and lightning strikes. Long-ago passersby wrote their names on it, and those needing help climbing the fascinating Chimney used to carve notches and drive sticks into it. One traveler walked around the base of the cone, just to measure, and counted 10,040 steps.

In the thick dust churned up by the fur traders' caravan, the missionaries traveled on. The mules pulled hard, getting them past Scott's Bluff, named, it is said, for an unlucky traveler whose bones were discovered there. Then over Roubidoux Pass.

Joseph Aspdin *invents portland cement, an improved hydraulic (hardens underwater) cement, which you have to have to make concrete.*	*A new ruler in Russia:* **Czar Nicholas I**		*February 29 —* *Although* **Andrew Jackson** *got slightly more votes,* **John Quincy Adams,** *son of President* **John Adams,** *is chosen to be 6th president. Jackson and his supporters are mad. Better luck next time (see 1828).*

Jedediah Smith, Jim Bridger, and many other mountain men had come this way. Later on, a multitude of Easterners would follow — 50,000 in 1852 alone — through Mitchell Pass, where some of the wagon ruts in the rock roadbed are still as much as eight feet deep! Well, it wasn't like that when Narcissa and her dusty fellow travelers came this way and finally got to Fort Laramie, on a Monday, June 13, 1836.

June 21 – July 18

From Laramie to the Green River Rendezvous

THEY RESTED AT FORT LARAMIE FOR A WEEK. Alfred Jacob Miller, a 27-year-old artist from Baltimore, Maryland, painted the busy trading post when he visited in 1837. He left us a pretty good idea of what the Whitmans and Spaldings saw when they arrived: a fort with a watchtower overlooking a courtyard, a place

March 27 — Charlottesville — Students begin classes at Virginia's new university, personally designed by **Thomas Jefferson**.

When hardly any women spoke in public, idealistic author **Frances Wright** *lectured American audiences on female equality and liberty for all. Now she founded Nashoba, an experimental farm in Tennessee where slaves could learn skills they'd need in freedom.*

of casual coming and going, it seems, for all sorts of prairie folks and their animals.

For Narcissa and Eliza, it was a chance to wash their clothes and see walls: a welcome sight after all the open spaces. Henry Spalding preached a sermon to the Indians and trappers who showed up at the Sunday service he conducted. Captain Fitzpatrick saw to it that his wagons were emptied and stored at the fort until he returned from the rendezvous with the year's fur harvest. As for the missionaries' Missouri farm wagon, it had gone as far as it would go. Pack mules, horses, and the Spaldings' blue and yellow wagon would be carrying the load on the next part of the journey. On the first day of summer, Narcissa and Eliza climbed into their sidesaddles, and once again, they were off.

A five-day ride got them about to where we'd find the modern city of Casper, Wyoming. What they found was ordeal. They had to cross the North Platte River. The animals could swim, but for the people and all that they were lugging, it was a complicated business. First, find willow branches. Bend them into boat skeletons. Unroll bundles of skins, which used to cover buffalo bulls. Stretch them over the willows so people can pile themselves and their luggage into these bull-boats and get to the other side.

1825

England —
George Stephenson's steam locomotive pulls the first passenger train.

October 25 —
Composer **Johann Strauss, Jr.,** "the Waltz King," is born in Vienna, Austria.

October 26 —
New York's Erie Canal is completed and open for business.

Now Tom Fitzpatrick led his caravan over 60 miles of tough, barren land to a huge, turtle-shaped granite rock almost a half-mile long and 193 feet high. Some say that he stashed some furs there on the Fourth of July, 1824. That's why he named it Independence Rock. On it would be scratched the names of hundreds of tired travelers who wanted to leave a record of themselves for whomever would come along after. Narcissa and her friends carved their names, too, so it's said, but maybe their autographs have been eroded away.

The caravan crossed a grassy valley and a pretty amazing time-space intersection: The South Pass, Independence Day, 1836. Its discovery in 1813 by Robert Stuart, one of John Jacob Astor's fur traders, was a big step in making the Oregon Trail possible. It was a direct way across the Continental Divide, America's backbone. A jug of water poured onto one side would make its slow way to the Gulf of Mexico and Atlantic Ocean. Pour it into the ground on the other side, and the water would flow to the Colorado or to the Snake and Columbia Rivers to the Pacific. Until that day, no female U.S. citizen had ever been where East truly meets West. It was such a big deal that Senator Lewis Linn made a speech in the Congress. Of course, he was a politician and

1826

Fur trapper **Jedediah Smith**, *in search of better trade routes, goes on an amazing adventure through western mountains and deserts.*

James Fenimore Cooper *writes* The Last of the Mohicans.

France — **Joseph Niépce** *invents photography. His method will be perfected by* **Louis Daguerre**, *who'll take lots of Daguerreotypes.*

eager for overlanders to settle in the Northwest so the U.S. would have a better chance at getting control over the Oregon Country away from Great Britain.

Far away in the United States, there were fireworks that night. Out where Narcissa and Marcus were camping, the night was blasted with the sound of horses running over the hills. Yells and whoops! Gunshots! A wild welcoming committee was all it was, from the mountain men's rendezvous, two days' ride away.

RENDEZVOUS ON THE GREEN

FITZPATRICK HAD SENT A RIDER to let them know they were almost there, to the annual fur trade fair. As traders and trappers had since 1825, they'd meet to swap pelts for money and goods wherever the grass was good for their horses, mules, and cattle. Then friends, families, and anyone passing through joined in the

1826

July 4 —
John Adams, *90, and*
Thomas Jefferson, *83,*
each pass away on the 50th
anniversary of Congress's
adoption of the Declaration
of Independence.

July 4 —
Pennsylvania —
Stephen Collins
Foster, *popular*
composer, is born.

Eugene Delacroix, *great*
artist of this romantic age,
paints "Greece Expiring on
the Ruins of Missolonghi"
to raise money for victims
of the Greek/Turkish war.

party. This year it was where Horse Creek met the Green River. Imagine hundreds of folks from the Flathead, Snake, Bannock, Nez Perce, Cayuse, and other tribes plus maybe 200 fur trappers and traders, all come to whoop it up. Maybe, since the fur trade was beginning to fade, the party wasn't as big, but this year, 1836, the rendezvous boasted a special, added attraction: a pair of white church ladies, like visitors from another planet.

"As soon as I alighted from my horse, I was met by a company of matrons, native women, one after the other, shaking hands and saluting me with a most hearty kiss," Narcissa wrote.

Welcome to the West!

"This was unexpected and affected me very much. They gave Sister Spalding the same salutation."

In a gentlemanly manner, the mountain men touched their fingertips to their hats. For a whole week, the women were

1827

John James Audubon *writes* Birds of North America.

March 26 — Composer **Ludwig van Beethoven**, *56, dies in Vienna.*

Japan — **Katsushika Hokusai**, *landscape painter, woodblock print-maker, is doing his greatest work.*

"in the midst of the gazing throng." Joe Meek told Narcissa about the bears he'd met in the wilds, and she put Bibles into eager hands. At the missionaries' worship services, grizzled mountain men gave plenty of attention to Narcissa's singing and her golden hair.

John and Richard would be going on west with the missionaries, but for now, after a year away, they rejoined their families with what joy and astonishing stories we can only imagine. Besides being a place for reuniting, partying, and doing business, the rendezvous was a chance for folks to send letters along with folks heading back East. Henry sent a progress report to the Mission Board. "We traveled 1,700 miles to Liberty mostly by water; 1,300 from Liberty to this place, all by land, and have yet 600 miles to make."

Like all the pioneers who would follow them down the Oregon Trail, the missionaries were awfully tired by now, and the worst of the journey was still ahead of them. They had an extra reason to be upset. The man they most wanted to see, the man who'd gone to scope out the Northwest for them, was nowhere to be seen. And, of course, they had no way of knowing that Samuel Parker was, right that minute, out on the blue Pacific. Marcus's tired, old traveling partner had decided to go home.

1827

Tennessee —
Humorous tall tale teller, author, frontiersman, and celebrity politician, **Davy Crockett** is elected to the U.S. Congress.

John Walker invents "Lucifers," friction matches (see 1836).

New York City —
John Brown Russwurm and **Samuel Cornish** begin Freedom's Journal, the nation's first newspaper to be owned and operated by blacks.

Boats would carry him by the Sandwich Islands, known these days as the Islands of Hawaii, then down around South America and up to New England.

Tom Fitzpatrick and his men were headed back to Missouri, so who would guide the two couples the rest of the way west? And where would they settle? With the Cayuse? Or the Nez Perce? Already the natives were quarreling over which tribe would get the white folks, each hoping that their presence, their "medicine," their black holy book, which they seemed to prize so highly, would help bring about some real world benefits. Perhaps the newcomers would provide new sources for trade goods. This was important now that the fur trade seemed to be slipping.

As for the missionaries, they were busting to get West with their Christian message. Already they'd heard tell of priests, a.k.a. "blackrobes," and others spreading Catholic teaching among Westerners, native and otherwise. Like lots of Protestants in their time, Narcissa and her buddies were wary of Catholic teaching. By 1844, when poor European Catholics were starting to fill America's big cities, the U.S. would even have an anti-Catholic, anti-foreigner political party. As it happened, the most influential missionary and peacemaker among the Indians was a stocky

1828

Robert Owen *had big ideas for social improvement. He did make life better for the workers in his Scottish mills. Now, from 1825 to 1828, he conducts a community experiment at New Harmony, IN, where perhaps a thousand "Owenites" share work, Mr. Owen's high ideals — try to, anyway — and their "village of cooperation."*

February 8 — **Jules Verne,** *science fiction author, is born in France.*

priest from Belgium, Father Pierre Jean De Smet. His 1841 trip on the Oregon Trail would be just one of his many trips into the West. De Smet, South Dakota, Laura Ingalls Wilder's little town on the prairie, was named after him. In any case, in 1836, the Whitmans, Spaldings, Cayuse, and Nez Perce all had high hopes. They were related but not identical.

Luckily, some Hudson Bay Company men came along and offered to guide the missionaries to Fort Hall. They'd be far to the south of the fiercer, more mountainous terrain that Lewis and Clark's Corps of Discovery had confronted 30-some years earlier. Still, it was a craggy country full of porcupines and the lava of old volcanoes, wickedly hard on the feet of animals and humans. They'd make their way to the Snake River, follow it to Fort Boise, then over the Blue Mountains to the trading post on the Walla Walla River, which fed into the mighty Columbia. Westward another 250 miles or so was Fort Vancouver, at the end of the Oregon Trail.

The Nez Perce as well as some Flathead and Snake folks decided that they'd come along, too, with the Whitmans, Spaldings, Richard, John, and the fur traders, if only part of the way. There was a long, long way to go.

1828

February 21 — *Georgia —* *Cherokees publish the* *first edition of the first* *Indian language* *newspaper:* The Cherokee Phoenix.	**Noah Webster** *writes his* American Dictionary of the English Language.	**Ranavalona I** *becomes queen* *of Madagascar.*		*July 15 —* **Jean Antoine Houdon**, *sculptor,* *dies in Paris.*

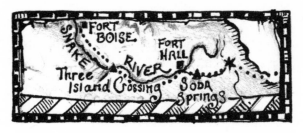

JULY 18 – AUGUST 19
Rendezvous (Wyoming) to Fort Boise (Idaho)

"DEAREST MOTHER," NARCISSA WROTE. "We commenced our journey to Walla Walla, July 18th, 1836, under the protection of Mr. McLeod, & his company..." Here is a sampling of her travel diary:

July 20. "Came twelve miles...over many steep & high mountains."

July 25. "Came fifteen miles today. Very mountainous. Paths winding on the sides of steep mountains. In some places the path is so narrow as scarcely to afford room for the animals to place his foot. One after another, we pass along with cautious steps....Husband has had a tedious time with the wagon today. Got [stuck] in the creek this morning...was obliged to wade considerably in getting it out. After that in going between two mountains, on the side of one so steep that it was difficult for

---

December 3 —
President John Quincy Adams *loses his bid for re-election to* **Andrew Jackson.**

December 22 —
Rachel Jackson, *wife of the president-elect, dies in Tennessee.*

Work begins on the Baltimore & Ohio, America's first passenger railroad.

horses to pass the wagon was upset twice. Did not wonder at this at all. It was a greater wonder that it was not turning a somerset [somersault] continually…"

July 26. "…Husband has been sick today…" No wonder!

July 27. "Our cattle endure this journey remarkably well. They are a source of great comfort to us in this land of scarcity. They supply us with milk for our tea & coffee…We have plenty of dry Buffalo meat…I can scarcely eat it, it appears so filthy…Do not think I regret coming. No; far from it. I would not go back for a world. I am contented & happy notwithstanding I get very hungry & weary. Have six weeks steady journeying before us…."

Everyone was sick and tired of wrestling the blue and yellow wagon up and down and over the rough trail, so much so that Narcissa was thrilled when it fell apart. Maybe the stubborn men would ditch it, but no. "They are making a cart of the hind wheels this afternoon & lashing the front wheels to it, intending to take it through in some shape or other."

Of course, on the trail to Oregon, there was more to the adventure than struggle. Like future overlanders, the Whitmans got a bang out of simply being tourists. They went to the Soda Springs and sipped the fizzy water. Lots of folks would write

1829

March 4 —
Andrew Jackson, *the Indian fighter, is still mourning his dead wife as he is sworn into office. Later, enthusiastic supporters so crowd the White House that the new president has to escape out a back window.*

David Walker, *a black man of North Carolina, urges slaves to fight for their freedom in his pamphlet, "An Appeal to the Colored Citizens of the World" (see 1830).*

Vienna —
Cyrillys Damien *invents the accordion.*

about the mineral springs thereabouts, named for their qualities. One tasted like beer; another puffed like a steamboat and shot up geysers of water. In 1852, a traveler tried to squelch one by sitting on the spring. Up and down he bobbed until he exclaimed, "Boys, there is no use trying to hold the devil down. It can't be did."

In later years, Soda Springs would be one of the turnoffs where some California-bound travelers would head their teams to the southwest, across the Nevada desert. Those who were going to Oregon went on up to Nathaniel Wyeth's trading post,

A refreshing pause

Fort Hall. The Boston ice seller-turned-fur trader built it in 1834 out of cottonwood logs and mud bricks. Now Joseph Thing, a hospitable Hudson Bay Company man, was in charge. Not only did he offer the travelers turnips from his struggling vegetable garden, he showed them rooms where they could sleep. Narcissa

1-2-3, 1-2-3 —
There's a sexy new dance craze in Europe's ballrooms — the waltz. It was popular earlier in the century, but it's really hot now.

February 26 —
Levi Strauss, *blue jeans manufacturing pioneer, is born in Germany.*

France, Russia, and Britain were for Greece. Egypt sided with the Turks, but at last, the Greeks win their independence.

and Marcus, Eliza and Henry slept under ceilings for the first time since leaving Missouri.

And they said good-bye to the Indians who'd been traveling with the caravan. Except for two of them, Kentuck and Chief Rottenbelly, they were heading to their home up north. By the way, it was a slow-healing wound that won *Tack-en-sua-tis*, a.k.a. Rottenbelly, his icky nickname.

Nothing at all like the wide, lazy Platte was the Snake River, boiling and blasting along between jagged walls of lava rock. Imagine August sun blazing down on hot dusty people, animals putting one sore hoof down after another, tails twitching at a misery of mosquitoes. Eliza Spalding's horse stepped into a hornet's nest. Thrown out of her sidesaddle, with her foot still stuck in its stirrup, she got dragged over rocky sand and sagebrush.

August 12. Marcus decided to lighten the wagon's load, and Narcissa wrote to her sister, "the little trunk you gave me has come with me so far...Poor little trunk, I am sorry to leave thee. Thou must abide here & no more by thy presence remind me of my Dear Harriet." Mr. McLeod offered to pack the "poor little trunk" onto one of the fur company's mules. What the mule thought of this gentlemanly offer was not recorded.

1829

June 27 —
British chemist, **James Smithson** dies and wills $500,000 for the founding of the scientific Smithsonian Institution in Washington, DC (see 1846).

September 15 —
Slavery is abolished in Mexico.

Gioacchino Antonio Rossini writes his last opera, William Tell. It includes a dandy overture.

India —
British rulers make the old Hindu custom of suttee illegal. No longer may a widow set herself on fire beside her husband's corpse. Some do anyway.

On and on they went, over the steep, rocky trail and over the river, but not before the cart and the poor mules were tangled and drenched in the waters of the cold Snake. It was an exhausted, bug-bitten crew who picked their way over the hard, stony country. Nerves were frayed. Marcus and Henry had argued more than once before the caravan rode into Fort Boise, where these days the Snake River makes itself into part of the Idaho/Oregon state line.

They rested, did their laundry, and hit the trail three days later — *without* the banged-up remains of Mrs. Spalding's wagon. Until then, no one had gotten anything with wheels so far west. Later on, of course, overlanders would get their sturdier wagons all the way west, but 'difficult' is too tame a word to describe their effort. The farther they traveled west, the more rugged was their path.

Years later, in 1845, Stephen Meek (Joe's brother) would guide more than 150 wagons as far as Fort Boise. He had hoped to bypass the terrible mountains up ahead. Thirst, injuries, and sickness killed 75 men, women, children, and who knows how many sore-footed oxen before Black Harris rescued them. Another fatal and far better known shortcut happened in 1846, but more about the dreadful Donner Party later on.

1830

Abolitionist pamphleteer **David Walker** is found dead. Poisoning is suspected.	**Louis Godey** publishes and **Sarah Josepha Hale** edits Godey's Lady's Book, first U.S. woman's magazine.	North Africa — France invades Algeria, which will not regain its independence until 1962, after many troubles.		April 6 — Fayette, NY — **Joseph Smith** organizes a Christian church of "Latter Day Saints," a.k.a. Mormons, for their belief in the Book of Mormon (see 1844).

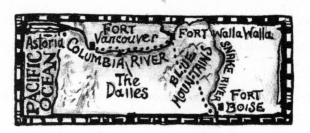

AUGUST 22 – SEPTEMBER 12
Fort Boise (Idaho) to Fort Vancouver (Washington)

WHEN RICHARD AND JOHN SWAM BEHIND THE CATTLE, all Narcissa could see were "so many heads floating upon the waters [of the Snake River.] Soon they gain the opposite shore, triumphantly ascend its banks [and] shake themselves." Rather than swim, the ladies had a treacherous ride in boats made of bullrushes and willows. Like future overlanders on the Oregon Trail, the missionaries, Nez Perce cowboys, and the fur company men headed north from the "Farewell Bend" of the winding Snake.

In the many years before it became firewood, a tall solitary pine tree, a living landmark, lorded over the vast valley near the Powder River. As future travelers would do, Narcissa and her husband rested by the Lone Tree, then came in sight of the hill

1830

<table>
<tr>
<td>May 1 —
Mary Harris Jones, a.k.a. "Mother Jones," labor organizer, activist for poor working men, women, and children, is born in Ireland.</td>
<td>With **President Jackson**'s enthusiastic support, the U.S. Congress passes the Indian Removal Act. All eastern tribes are to be moved west.</td>
<td></td>
<td>July 15 —
Chief **Black Hawk** is against it, but the Fox and Sauk tribes cede (hand over) their lands east of the Mississippi River (see 1832).</td>
</tr>
</table>

leading to the Grande Ronde. Here's how Narcissa described it: "It is a circular plain surrounded by lofty mountains." A stream threaded through the round valley where Indians came to gather huckleberries, a favorite of future overlanders, and camas. These bulbs looked like onions "in shape & color," Narcissa recorded, and "when cooked is very sweet, tastes like a fig." Camas roots, baked in the ground under heated stones or made into bread, were a big part of the Indians' wintertime menus.

After dinner, the travelers set out to conquer the terrible Blue Mountains. At first the tree-covered hills reminded Narcissa of home in New York, and there was good grass for the animals. Before long though, they began going up and down "one of the most terrible mountains for steepness...it was like winding stairs ...& in some places almost perpendicular...the horses appeared to dread the hill as much as we did." Black, broken volcanic rock covered much of their path. "We had no sooner gained the foot of this mountain when another more steep & dreadful was before us."

Scary it was, but so beautiful. "Just as we gained the highest elevation...the sun was dipping his disk behind the western horizon. Beyond the valley we could see two distant Mountains: Mount Hood & Mount St. Helens."

August 28 —
Tom Thumb, *the first American-built steam locomotive, is shown off by its builder,* **Peter Cooper**.

September 15 —
The Choctaw people cede their Alabama and Mississippi lands. The Choctaw, Cherokee, Creek, Seminole, and Chickasaw are called the "Five Civilized Tribes" because they'd adopted some European ways. Nevertheless, they are destined for the new Indian Territory (Oklahoma). Thousands of Choctaw die on their way there.

The fur company men shaved. Narcissa must have been amused at the sight of the tough men washing their shirts and

Frontier travelers getting tidied up

"some are cutting their hair," getting ready for their arrival at Fort Walla Walla. According to frontier custom, they sent a rider on to the trading post to let folks know company was coming. Here in the future, we know what Narcissa and Marcus did not: Their future home was just a few miles away. Pierre Pambrun, the French Canadian clerk, came out to meet them and escort them all into the fort.

Eating bread and butter, salmon, potatoes, and a "feast of mellons." Meeting Pierre's wife, Maria, who could speak both

1830

London —
The Royal Geographical Society is founded to promote exploration and study of the world.

Paris —
Parisians revolt against too aristocratic **Charles X**. He's replaced by "Citizen King" **Louis Philippe**, who'll be even more unpopular and booted out in the 1848 revolution.

October 24 —
Belva Lockwood, first woman lawyer to practice before the Supreme Court, is born in New York. She'll be the first female presidential candidate, too.

French and the language of her Indian relatives. Seeing and hearing hogs, goats, clucking hens, and crowing rooster. Sleeping in a bed indoors. It was all a wonder after so many months of frontier camping. Everyone and all but two broken-down horses plodded into the fort on September 3, 1836. Two other horses were lost or stolen along the way, and of the original 17 cattle, 8 made it to Walla Walla. In her diary, Narcissa thanked "a kind Providence." There was still much to do before they could begin their work. Their journey wasn't over, but their overland trip was done.

Arriving at Fort Walla Walla

1831

December 10 —
Emily Dickinson, *poet,*
is born in Massachusetts.

December 29 —
Ezra Meeker, *champion*
of the Oregon Trail,
is born in Ohio.

January 1 — Boston —
William Lloyd
Garrison *publishes*
his first Liberator,
an anti-slavery
newspaper.

August 21 — Virginia —
Powerful preacher **Nat Turner**
launches a slave revolt. Sixty
whites, including Turner's
owner, are killed. In the end,
100 innocent slaves are killed.
On November 11, Turner and
his 16 followers are hanged.

THE REST OF THE WAY

THE SPALDINGS, THE WHITMANS, MR. GRAY, AND MR. PAMBRUN piled into a 30-foot-long open boat along with the fellow who worked the rudder. Six Iroquois men at the oars and six days down the Columbia would bring them to Fort Vancouver. In later years, loads of emigrants on the Oregon Trail would travel the rough, south bank of the river. Near such Oregon towns as Echo and Cecil you can still find ruts in the earth from the overlanders' patched and battered wagons.

Narcissa Whitman went boating on a very different river from today's Columbia, which pushes through 14 big hydroelectric dams, all busily turning the river into reservoirs and a magnificent irrigating, electricity-making machine. Narcissa saw waters "clear as crystal & smooth as a sea of glass, exceeding in beauty the Ohio of the east. But," she recorded, "the scenery on each side

1831

Virginia —
For faster grain harvesting, **Cyrus McCormick** invents a reaper.

With magnets and coiled copper wire, two scientists come closer to tapping the power of electricity. Both England's **Michael Faraday** and **Joseph Henry** of the U.S. discover the principle of electromagnetic induction.

Charles Darwin sails on the H.M.S. Beagle on a five-year scientific expedition through the South Pacific Ocean.

is very different. No timber to be seen. High perpendicular banks or rocks in some places, rugged bluffs and plains of sand is all that greets the eye."

They set up their tents of an evening on the treeless shore, built fires, and Mr. Pambrun's cook rustled up dinner. (Unlike future pioneer women, Narcissa and Eliza didn't do much cooking on the trail.) Sometimes, when the Columbia was too wild for boating, as when the river flung itself over the Chutes, they walked. A great place for salmon fishing the Chutes were, for timeless generations of bears and people, but impossible for rafts and canoes. Later, these falls were called the Celilo; still later, they vanished under the lake made by the Dalles Dam.

In return for twists of tobacco, 20 Indians *portaged* (carried) the boat; still others lugged the baggage around the Chutes or, a little farther on, past the Dalles. Narcissa saw the treacherous river surging between "two rocks, of immense size & height... with great rapidity." Farther still, she and the others would have to get around the Cascade rapids, now long gone under the Bonneville Dam reservoir.

In the years to come, multitudes would travel the long trail into the West. By the time they reached the wild Columbia, they'd

1832

Chloroform is discovered.

January 6 — Boston — The New England Anti-Slavery Society is formed.

Boston — The nation's first school for the blind opens.

January 27 — **Charles Dodgson,** *author of Alice in Wonderland (under the name of* **Lewis Carroll***), is born in England.*

New Yorkers get their first ride in horse-drawn trolleys.

covered almost 1,800 miles. Most were headed farther on, to the rich farmland along the Willamette River. To get there, they'd sell their half-dead oxen or whatever they had to buy passage down the Columbia River. All too often, exhausted travelers met death in its waters, just when he or she had almost made it. Later on, they could avoid the river by struggling over a truly horrible toll road ($5 per wagon). Sam Barlow and Joel Palmer made the road by hacking through the fierce landscape around Mount Hood.

At this point in Narcissa Whitman's adventure, her greatest worries were fleas! Crawling all over her! Until they could change their clothes, every squirming person in the boat brushed at these "miserable companions." And after this insect invasion, she got her first upsetting glimpse of an old tradition.

A proud Chinook mother showed the missionaries how she was shaping her baby's head in what Narcissa called a "pressing machine." The mom put a little cushion on the infant's forehead, wrapped a bandage tightly around, pressing its head against the board, pillowed with a squirrel skin. In only three or four months, the baby's head would be formed forever into the fashionable shape admired by upper class Chinook people. Everyone — everyone but some visiting white newcomers, that

1832

November 26 —
Dr. Mary Edwards Walker, *reformer, only woman to receive the Congressional Medal of Honor, the highest military award, is born in New York.*

November 29 —
Louisa May Alcott, *author of* Little Women, *is born in Massachusetts.*

Northern IL — Sauk *and Fox Indians try and fail to take back part of their land. Young* **Abe Lincoln** *joined a troop of settlers, but he saw no action in the Black Hawk War.*

Fashion can be painful.

is — would know by its flattened head that this child was no slave or otherwise stuck on the lower rungs of society's ladder. To Narcissa and her companions, the baby was merely pitiful.

Ah well. They were told that the custom was wearing away, and anyway, new experiences awaited the wandering missionaries. Here they were at Fort Vancouver, "the New York of the Pacific Ocean." They'd arrived.

1833

Kinder, gentler labor laws in London: Factory owners shall not hire children younger than 9. Kids between 9 and 13 shall not spend more than 9 hours a day on the job.

Felix Mendelssohn *writes his* Italian Symphony.

August 1 — Slavery is abolished all through the British Empire.

King Ferdinand VII *dies and his two-year-old daughter,* **Isabella,** *is queen — but her uncle wants the throne and Spaniards are divided. There will be fighting and trouble for years.*

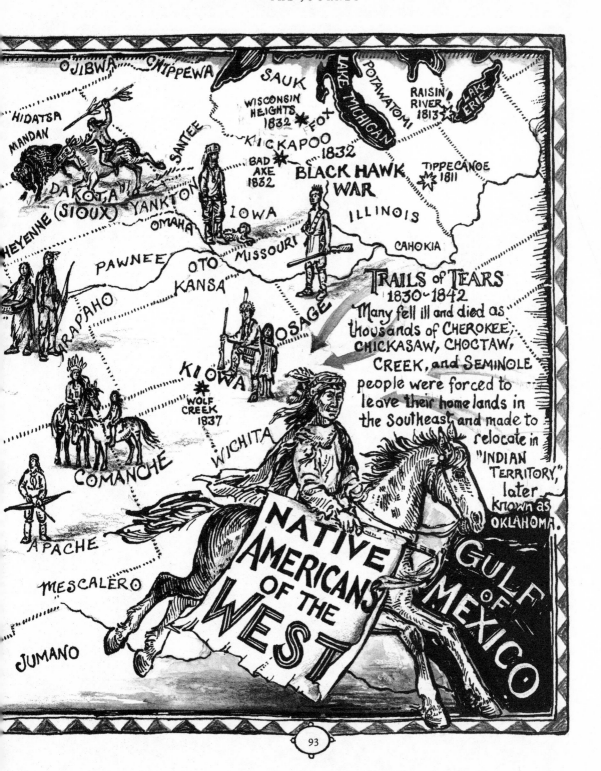

OJIBWA · CHIPPEWA

SAUK

WISCONSIN HEIGHTS 1832

FOX

KICKAPOO 1832

BAD AXE 1832

BLACK HAWK WAR

POTAWATOMI

RAISIN RIVER 1813

LAKE ERIE

LAKE MICHIGAN

TIPPECANOE 1811

HIDATSA

MANDAN

SANTEE

DAKOTA (SIOUX) YANKTON

IOWA

ILLINOIS

CHEYENNE

OMAHA

MISSOURI

CAHOKIA

PAWNEE

OTO

KANSA

ARAPAHO

OSAGE

KIOWA

WOLF CREEK 1837

COMANCHE

WICHITA

TRAILS of TEARS 1830~1842
Many fell ill and died as thousands of CHEROKEE, CHICKASAW, CHOCTAW, CREEK, and SEMINOLE people were forced to leave their homelands in the Southeast and made to relocate in "INDIAN TERRITORY," later known as OKLAHOMA.

APACHE

MESCALERO

JUMANO

NATIVE AMERICANS OF THE WEST

GULF OF MEXICO

CHAPTER FOUR

The Oregon Country

THE FATHER OF OREGON

A painting on the wall of Oregon's State Capitol shows that historic Monday morning, September 12, 1836. Narcissa Whitman and her companions are greeting a tall, dignified man, stern looking and formally dressed. A lion's mane of white hair fans around his face in which pale eyes gleam out of deep-set sockets. He is Dr. John McLoughlin. To many natives of this part of the world, he is the White-headed Eagle. To his employer, the Hudson Bay Company (HBC), he is Chief Factor (superintendent) of Fort Vancouver, the HBC's trading post at

1833

September 1 —
Benjamin Day introduces the first penny newspaper, the New York Sun.

Philadelphia —
Lucretia Mott starts a Female Anti-Slavery Society.

New York —
John Matthews opens the first soda fountain.

Artist **Ando Hiroshige** creates a charming series of woodblock color prints called "Fifty-three Stages on the Tokaido," the road between Edo (where Tokyo is now) and Kyoto, Japan.

the mouth of the Columbia River. To future generations, he'll be known as the Father of Oregon. Why? Because these missionaries are not the first and absolutely will not be the last bunch of tired-out newcomers he will welcome into the Pacific Northwest.

Dr. McLoughlin ruled a complex corporate empire, involving international shipping, trappers, traders, native tribes, and foreign governments, all taking part in the worldwide buying and selling of furs. Did he and the HBC want thousands of uninvited American settlers dragging into the wild Oregon Country — still partly controlled by the British crown, don't forget — plowing, chopping, and scaring off what was left of the beavers? Strengthening the U.S. claim on this part of the continent? Certainly not! But the missionaries were "worn out by fatigue, hardships and danger," as McLoughlin noted later. For them and those who'd come after, he was determined to do what he believed to be right. He'd help those who came to his door with seeds, credit, shelter, and advice. Later on, this sort of hospitality at his company's expense will get him fired, but then, in September 1836, the Whitmans and Spaldings were happy to be met by the White-headed Eagle and to find a haven at the end of the trail. Then they were very upset. Where on earth was Reverend Parker?

1834

London — **Madame Marie Tussaud** *opens a permanent exhibition of her wax works.*

Davy Crockett *writes his autobiography,* A Narrative of the Life of David Crockett, of the State of Tennessee.

Massachusetts — **Jacob Perkins**'s *new compression machine leads to modern mechanical refrigerators.*

They thought that Marcus's old traveling buddy and missionary recruiter would be there to help them get started. Instead, Parker had sailed away home (remember?), leaving behind, it seems, precious little advice. And there was another fateful wrinkle in the missionaries' plans. Marcus and Henry had already come to a fateful decision: They meant to set up not one but two missions, one with the Cayuse, the other in Nez Perce lands.

Each tribe wanted its own teacher from the East, bringing spiritual wisdom as well as good insider information on rich, high-tech white civilization. McLoughlin and others warned Dr. Whitman against settling with the cantankerous Cayuse, but Marcus was stubborn. Good men though they were, he and Henry had argued more than once, and Spalding's long-ago broken romance with Narcissa didn't help matters any. Dangerous though the West surely could be, it was at least plenty big enough for a pair of competitive men to spread out and not work in each other's shadow if they didn't feel like it.

Meanwhile, their wives stayed in the tiny, cosmopolitan community of Fort Vancouver, safely surrounded by a huge, stockade, 20 feet tall. To Eliza, the fort's dairy, chapel, barns, library, orchards, and gardens abounded with the "luxuries of life."

1835

Mexico — **General Antonio Lopez de Santa Anna** *defeats* **Emperor Agustin de Interbide** *and makes himself dictator.*

England — The **Tolpuddle Martyrs,** *six poor workers from the village of Tolpuddle, are sent by authorities to a prison colony in Australia for seven years. Their crime? Trying to start a trade union.*

Hartford, CT — **Samuel Colt** *patents the first successful repeating pistol.*

At its stores and workshops, she and Mrs. Whitman bought supplies and tools for their missions. They helped out in its school, where Narcissa taught new songs to the "50 scholars... who have French fathers and Indian mothers & many orphans." Some days they went riding with Mrs. McLoughlin, a part Cree Indian lady. She and the other women in the fort straddled their horses "gentleman fashion" and encouraged Narcissa and Eliza to do the same, but no thanks. They preferred their ladylike sidesaddles.

Between the tough journey from the East and the years ahead of her, the weeks at Fort Vancouver were a civilized oasis

An oasis on the frontier

for Narcissa Whitman. Still, she was eager to get settled in a home of her own with her husband. Winter storms were around the corner, and with the spring would come a new baby.

1835

P. T. Barnum's *first successful hoax: he exhibits* **Joice Heth** *as* **George Washington's** *161-year-old nursemaid. In truth Joice was only about 80.*

Alexis de Toqueville *writes* Democracy in America, *about this French philosopher's 7,000-mile trip through the U.S.*

Osceola *and the Seminole Indians hide in the Everglades and fight a hard seven years, winning several battles, if not the war, to keep their Florida homeland (see 1838).*

DISAPPOINTMENTS AT WAIILATPU, WHERE THE RYE GRASS GROWS

IF WE JUMPED AHEAD INTO NARCISSA'S FUTURE, a few years closer to our present, we'd find her and Marcus living close by the Walla Walla River in a whitewashed adobe house. Their mission was called *Waiilatpu*, meaning "place of the people of the rye grass." Six days ride to the east, in modern Idaho, was the Spaldings' home at *Lapwai*, "place of the butterflies." The Whitman's home was a far cry from the cottonwood-and-mud-brick hut Marcus and Mr. Gray built that first winter. After one or two floods, the permanent house was built, larger, higher, and farther from the Walla Walla. Not too far away was a cluster of Cayuse longhouses.

Western travelers might see the Whitmans' mills for grinding grain and sawing logs, smokehouse, corn crib, blacksmith shop, and storehouses as well as fruit trees, chickens, cattle, horses,

Gaetano Donizetti *writes the tragic opera* Lucia di Lammermoor.

October 2 — Gonzales — American colonists fight and win the first battle of the Texas revolutionary war for independence from Mexico.

November 30 — author **Samuel Clemens,** *a.k.a.* **Mark Twain,** *is born in Missouri.*

99

and hogs. A flock of sheep dotted the pastures. Corn and wheat grew on 30 farmed and irrigated acres, mostly thanks to the efforts of Walla Walla Indians and *Kanakas* (Hawaiian workers imported from the Sandwich Islands).

The Cayuse, as the Whitmans came to see them, were too proud and lazy to work.

Actually, the Cayuse were pretty busy, raising and trading horses and otherwise keeping body and soul together. Each spring, they moved from the longhouses in their winter villages to mountain meadows and favorite fishing spots, far from the puzzled, puzzling missionaries. There was food gathering, preserving, and hunting to do as well as the making of clothes, baskets, and other necessities. They danced. They visited, and, doing so, they gave and received presents. People such as the Whitmans, who did not exchange gifts, seemed rather rude and stuck-up to the Cayuse. The missionaries, in turn, did not approve of gambling, which the Cayuse loved to do whenever they raced their magnificent horses. As for the time-honored practice of men having more than one wife, you can imagine what Narcissa thought of that!

Around the fires in their longhouses, the Cayuse swapped stories. Some told about the world's creation and the sacred

1835   **1836**

Hans Christian Andersen *publishes his first fairy tale. It will be followed by 167 more.*

January 10 — **Charles "Pa" Ingalls,** *father of* **Laura Ingalls Wilder** *(future author of books about her pioneer life), is born in Cuba, New York.*

South Africa — *To escape British settlers, Dutch Boers go on the Great Trek farther north, leading to more trouble, bloodshed, and death as British and Dutch clash with native Bantu and Zulu peoples.*

Telling old stories on a full-moon night

mother all around them, her hair in the waving grasses, her bones in the rocks and stones. She was the giver of nature's gifts, animals, trees, mountains and such, each with its holy spirit. The Cayuse people were happy to add Christian songs, prayers, and Sabbath-keeping to their holy rituals, but they never expected to have to give up their own religion and way of life, for heaven's sake.

March 6 – San Antonio, TX –
For 12 days, **General Santa Anna** and 5,000 Mexican soldiers bombard the old mission known as the Alamo before they storm its walls. The 187 men inside, including **William B. Travis**, **James Bowie**, and **Davy Crockett**, defend the Alamo and Texan independence to the death.

March 27 – Texas –
General Santa Anna and his men kill more than 300 Texans at the **Battle of Goliad**. Was this the end of the Texan war for independence?

Eliza's stairway to heaven

As the missionaries understood their job, they needed to get a person to fully understand and accept the Christian faith and show a big change of heart and behavior. Only then could they report to the churchmen in Boston that an individual had been baptized and a soul had been saved. But concepts such as forgiveness and Jesus dying to save mankind from sin were complicated. Many an experienced Christian could argue and discuss these ideas all day and all night. Even with Richard interpreting, it was hard to explain these ideas in Nez Perce, a language often used by the Cayuse.

Besides being better at speaking with and understanding their native neighbors, the Spaldings used pictures. Eliza illustrated a chart with Bible stories, such as Adam and Eve and Jesus on his cross. At the top of her six-foot-tall "learning ladder" was

1836

April 21 —
General Santa Anna *is captured and his army is defeated by* **Sam Houston**'s *outnumbered fighters, who shout "Remember the Alamo!" Texas is now an independent republic.*

Santa Anna

Massachusetts —
Alonzo D. Phillips *invents phosphorus matches. Improved "safety" matches come along in 1844.*

June 15 —
Arkansas is the Union's 25th state.

an angel-filled heaven, its pathway blocked, by the way, by the pope. Eliza and her companions were well aware of Catholic competition for Indian hearts and minds. Intrepid, black-robed priests also used visual aids. Theirs showed non-Catholics falling into the eternal flames. For the uninitiated, it all must have been pretty confusing.

"They feel so bad, disappointed, and some of them angry," Narcissa wrote about the Cayuse in 1840 in a letter to her mom, "because husband tells them that none of them are Christians; that they are all of them in the broad road to destruction....They try to persuade him not to talk such bad talk to them, as they say, but talk good talk, or tell some story....Some threaten to whip him and to destroy our crops....These things did not intimidate us."

But when it came to her neighbors, other things did, for a fact, get her down.

"The greatest trial to a woman's feelings is to have her cooking and eating room always filled with four or five or more Indians — men — especially at meal time," she wrote. "We have a room there we devote to them especially, and shall not permit them to go into the other part of the house at all. They are so filthy they make a great deal of cleaning wherever they go, and this wears out a woman very fast."

1837

September 14 —
Aaron Burr, Thomas Jefferson's old Vice President, scoundrel, and killer of founding father **Alexander Hamilton** in an 1804 duel, dies in New York.

Zimbabwe —
The Rozwi people's Changamire empire is attacked and taken over by the Ngoni, led by fierce female general **Nyamazana**.

Sitting Bull, Hunkpapa Sioux medicine man and leader, is born in present-day South Dakota.

Charles Dickens writes Oliver Twist.

For his part, energetic, stubborn Marcus refused to be discouraged, even when a frustrated Cayuse hit him or when men forced their way into his house in which they were not made welcome. But this fine house was on Cayuse land for which the white folks had paid no money. For their part, the Whitmans figured that they'd been invited. And why should Marcus's lady frown when they looked in at her fine glass windows or walked in without knocking? Even the sight of all of their cloth garments drying on the clothesline stirred resentment. It was as if these so-called "Bostons" were displaying their wealth. The Cayuse and the missionaries were pretty disappointed in each other.

As for Narcissa Whitman, gone was the confident bride bound for Western adventure. Life had changed her, there behind her green-shuttered windows, closed to prying eyes. What would this proper housewife have said, if she could, to her romantic teenage self back in New York, reading and daydreaming about noble missionary work? Might she have warned her about loneliness? Two years or more could pass between the time a Westerner wrote to a dear one back East and got a letter in return. Mail traveled in an overlander's pouch or in ships sailing down around the tip of South America and up again.

1837

England —
William F. Cooke and
Charles Wheatstone *invent*
an electromagnetic telegraph
(see 1840).

January 26 —
Michigan becomes the 26th state.

To turn over
and break up
the prairie sod,
John Deere
invents his
steel plow.

March 4 —
Martin van Buren
becomes the 8th president.
People will have a rotten
time of it during his
administration, as the
U.S. slides into an
economic depression.

Martin Van Buren

Self-doubt? There were times when Narcissa felt "entirely unfitted" for her job. "I desire to be cheerful," she wrote in 1844, "because it is a duty; but I find it hard work always to be so, especially when husband was gone." And Marcus was often away, tending his patients and mission work.

Sickness and frustration? Narcissa's health really was dreadful from time to time, but she was not above taking to her bed rather than deal with the frustrating Cayuse or the four pairs of newlywed missionaries that the Board sent West in 1838, for reinforcements. Most were greenhorns with no more idea than this author of how to live in the wilderness. At crowded Waiilatpu, they got on each other's nerves something awful. Still, these pioneer wives created the region's very first women's organization, the Columbia Maternal Association. However isolated they were to be, as they eventually went their separate ways (*see page 106*), they'd share their studies in letters. They'd pray and meditate, uniting their brain waves at a regular time everyday. It was a way to be a community.

Mrs. Whitman could have had lots to say to her younger self about deep sorrow and disappointment of the kind she felt when the Whitmans' two-year-old daughter, Alice Clarissa, died

1838

November 7 —
A proslavery mob in Alton, Illinois, murders abolitionist newspaperman **Elijah P. Lovejoy** and pitches his printing press into the Mississippi River.

Ohio —
Oberlin becomes the nation's first coeducational college.

January 4 —
Charles Sherwood Stratton is born in Connecticut. As a 40-inch-tall adult, he will be world famous as circus showman **General Tom Thumb**.

in 1839. The Cayuse wondered how it was that these Bostons, who claimed to follow God's true path, were powerless when it came to saving a much-loved child from drowning in the Walla Walla. Days went by before Narcissa would let the child's body be put into the ground. Years went by, and she never buried her sadness.

"The Lord has taken our own dear child away," Narcissa wrote in March 1842, "so that we may care for the poor outcasts of the country," such as black-haired, stubborn Helen, Joe Meek's two-year-old daughter. Jim Bridger, too, brought his mild, six-year-old daughter, Mary Ann, to be cared for and educated at Waiilatpu. Both girls had Indian mothers. A half-starved Spanish-Indian two-year-old was brought to the Whitmans in 1842. "I could not shut my heart against him," Narcissa wrote. She named the toddler David Malin, after a friend back East. Two years later, she and Marcus opened their hearts to seven more children. More about them later.

Narcissa threw herself into housekeeping, mothering, and teaching, skills she'd learned from her own mother. Like her, Narcissa was strict. As for the job that she was sent to do — converting her native neighbors to Christianity — nothing had prepared her and Marcus for that. Hardly any Cayuse had

1838

Second Seminole War — In 1837, when **Asiyaholo**, a.k.a. **Osceola**, Creek Indian warrior, went to talk peace terms under a white truce flag, soldiers took him prisoner. He died in U.S. custody, January 30, 1838.

June 28 — Coronation of **Queen Victoria**. She'll reign throughout the century, which became known as the Victorian Age.

become, in the eyes of the Whitmans, a proper Christian. They chose instead to be proper Cayuse, as they themselves saw fit. Besides, they had worries of their own, what with more and more white settlers showing up with each passing year. The more flexible Spaldings did better with the Nez Perce, but only slightly.

The churchmen at the Board worried when they read letters full of the Oregon missionaries' complaints and concerns about each other. When the Board's answer arrived, by way of the 1842 wagon train, the missionaries had an emergency meeting.

DR. WHITMAN'S GREAT ADVENTURE

WHAT HAPPENED NEXT IN THIS WESTERN SAGA had a lot to do with what was happening back East. The Whitmans and Spaldings represented loads of Americans who wanted there to be a strong Protestant Christian presence in the West. If these numbers were

1838

The Trail of Tears, 1838–39 — Thousands die when U.S. troops force-march Cherokee men, women, and children from their lands in America's Southeast to Indian Territory (Oklahoma).

December 16 — In South Africa, Boers kill 3,000 Zulus at the Battle of Blood River.

not to be converted Indians — not likely, considering the missionaries' rate of success — then the best hope lay in white pioneers coming over the mountains. On top of this was a patriotic, sea-to-shining-sea notion beginning to take hold in America: The more U.S. settlers there were in the Pacific Northwest, the more likely it was that their nation would take control of it.

Already, in 1841, Tom Fitzpatrick and Joe Meek had guided the first genuine, organized wagon train out from Missouri. Folks called it the "Bidwell-Bartleson Party," after the the names of its captains. This train split up along the way, half of the pioneers bound for Oregon, the rest barely surviving a terrible trip to California. More than a hundred people came West in 1842. Certainly even more would be setting out next season.

Now, with so much change and movement in the wind, the churchmen were firing the Spaldings, ordering them back to the States? Yes. Moreover, they wanted the Whitmans to close Waiilatpu and go work with the other missionary couples up at Tshimakain, far north of the overlanders' trail.

Stubborn, determined Marcus saddled up his horse and got ready for a drastic, dangerous journey. He'd talk to the churchmen in Boston face to face, and to the politicians in Washington!

1839

Opium War 1839–1842 —
China sold tea and silk, but it bought hardly any western goods. To balance things out, European merchants made money by sneaking the profitable drug opium into China. When the Chinese tried to stop this, Britain and China went to war. The English win the war and control of the island-city of Hong Kong for the next 99 years.

July — Cuban waters — **Joseph Cinquez,** *a.k.a.* **Cinque,** *a kidnapped African, leads a revolt on the slave ship Amistad. He and others are charged with piracy (see 1841).*

Marcus meets Daniel Webster
(center) and President Tyler

An adventurous fellow named Asa Lovejoy, a lawyer by trade, volunteered to tackle the trip with Dr. Whitman. By October 3, 1842, Marcus, Lovejoy, and the Whitmans' dog, Trapper, were on their way to the United States of America.

It was a gaunt, frostbitten frontiersman who showed up in Washington, D.C., almost six months later. Marcus Whitman had gotten lost, he'd staggered through blinding white storms, and nearly drowned in the freezing Colorado River. If it hadn't been for the pack mules and, sad to say, Trapper the dog, he and Lovejoy would have starved in the snowy mountains north of Taos in present-day New Mexico.

In the spring of 1843, Marcus in his worn-out furs and buckskins must have cut quite a figure as he met with bigshots in the marble halls of the nation's government. Because

1839

September 28 —
Frances E. Willard, *reformer, is born in New York.*

Until 1842, Afghanistan people fight off British invaders.

Charles Goodyear *figures out how to vulcanize rubber, making it stronger and stretchier.*

Cooperstown, NY—
According to legend, **Abner Doubleday** *lays out a diamond and invents baseball this year.*

Americans were focusing on the lands beyond the Rocky Mountains, President John Tyler and Daniel Webster, the illustrious Secretary of State, were eager to hear from Dr. Whitman, someone who'd been there. For his part, Marcus wanted what Oregon boosters in the Congress were already talking about: land grants for would-be pioneers, a frontier peppered with posts where food was raised for the overlanders and soldiers were quartered to protect the wagon trains. In his mind, he saw fresh horses at these frontier posts so couriers could carry the mail clear out to the Pacific Ocean. Of course, here in the distant future, we know what Marcus never would, that in 1860–61, 17 years after he imagined it, there really would be a Pony Express.

Up in New York, Marcus talked up Oregon with the famous newspaper editor Horace Greeley. Then, in Boston he appalled his bosses. How, the churchmen wondered, had one of their missionaries turned into this tattered tramp in moccasins, and why had he left Oregon without their permission? But they heard him out and agreed, in the end, that he and Narcissa and Henry and Eliza must stay at their missions, ministering to the natives and to the white pioneers sure to be coming their way.

1840

Scottish blacksmith **Kirkpatrick Macmillan** *builds the first real bicycle — with foot pedals.*

U.S. population: 17,069,453 people

May 27 —
*Death of superstar **Niccolo Paganini**, who fiddled so fantastically that some said he must've made a deal with the devil*

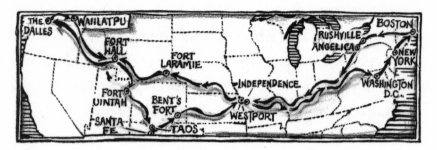

Dr. Whitman's amazing adventure

As quickly as stagecoaches and muddy roads permitted, Marcus traveled across New York State to see his and Narcissa's families. He hurried away again and with him went a young nephew who begged to go West. Like many other Americans, Uncle Marcus and 13-year-old Perrin Whitman had caught the "Oregon Fever."

That spring of 1843, as many as 1,000 travelers and 120 wagons were gathering at the Missouri end of the Oregon Trail, waiting for the prairie to green up enough to feed the livestock legions. Foreboding and homesickness there must have been, but plenty were busting to get going. They wanted to "see the elephant" with their own eyes: They wanted to experience the big deal, the main attraction for themselves. Marcus, on his mule, would help to lead this milling, mooing conglomeration on

1840

England —
People call them "Penny Blacks," the first adhesive postage stamp out this year. It has a picture of young **Queen Victoria** *(newly wed in February to Prince Albert).*

London —
Lucretia Mott *and* **Elizabeth Cady Stanton** *are furious. They can't take part in the World Anti-Slavery Convention because their spirits inhabit female bodies. Seeds for a woman's equality movement are planted.*

wheels, hoofs, and shoe leather, the biggest wagon train so far. Marcus tended the sick by night, looked for the best routes by day, and hurried the caravan along. Cattle herder Jesse Applegate would remember his cheerful advice: "Travel, travel, TRAVEL. Nothing else will take you to the end of your journey."

Lord Stewart, the adventuring Scotsman who'd gone along with Tom Fitzpatrick's 1836 caravan, was just one of the colorful characters out on the Trail that season, along with Peter Burnett, California's future first governor, and a 39-year-old mule driver Baptiste Charbonneau, son of Lewis and Clark guide Sacagawea.

The Great Emigration heads out of Independence, Missouri.

Washington, DC —
Inventor/painter
Samuel F. B. Morse
patents his telegraph,
for which he's designed
a dot-dash code.

November 14 —
Claude Monet,
painter, is born
in Paris.

Navigator/explorer
Charles Wilkes
scientifically proves
the existence of the
Antarctic continent
by sailing clear
around it.

Future presidential candidate John Charles Frémont, his guide Kit Carson, and cartographer Charles Preuss were out exploring. Together they'd help produce the first scientific map of the American West.

Explorer Frémont and his fellow travelers

Along the way, Asa Lovejoy joined up with the dusty migration, rattling and creaking down the Oregon Trail. Painted on many a canvas cover were bumper sticker slogans such as 'Oregon or Bust!', 'Prairie Bird', 'Never Say Die!', 'Red Rover', or "Sweet Sallie." Every turn of the wheel brought the wagons closer to the treacherous Rockies, the Blue Mountains, and the dreadful Cascades. Mile after mile they went, fording creeks and rivers, pushing, pulling, hauling their rigs up the mountains and letting them down

1841

March 4 —
William Henry Harrison *becomes the 9th president of the U.S.*

March 9 —
U.S. Supreme Court: **John Quincy Adams** *represents* **Cinque,** *who led the Amistad takeover. He and the others are found not guilty and allowed to return to Africa (see 1839).*

April 4 —
President Harrison *dies.* **Vice President John Tyler** *takes over as the 10th president.*

with ropes, pulleys, and pure, brute muscle, human and animal.

The wonder is that most of the travelers made it and were proud for the rest of their lives to have done so. Marcus Whitman certainly was. He wrote about it later on. "I am happy to have been the means of landing so large an emigration on the shores of the Columbia, with their wagons, families and stock, all in safety....It does not concern me so much what is to become of any particular set of Indians....I have no doubt our greatest work is to be to aid the white settlement of this country and to help to found its religious institutions."

A week after her husband left, Narcissa had gone off on an unexpected trip of her own, to Fort Walla Walla, after a sound at her bedroom door awakened her in the night.

"I sprang from the bed in a moment and closed the door again, but the ruffian pushed and pushed and tried to unlatch it." Whoever it was ran away when she called for help, but except for one brief return visit, she and her foster children spent the next year far from Waiilatpu, staying, mostly, with the Methodist missionaries at the Dalles. That's where she and Marcus reunited on October 26, 1843, after more than a year apart. The Whitmans went back to Waiilatpu and began the last chapter of their lives.

Oregon Country —
Chief Umtippe
of the Cayuse dies.

New York City —
Curiosity-seekers crowd into
P. T. Barnum's *new American Museum to see plays and people such as the famous twins* **Chang** *and* **Eng**, *conjoined since their births in Siam (Thailand).*

Edgar Allan Poe,
inventor of the detective story, writes Murders in the Rue Morgue.

CHAPTER FIVE

Destiny

*"For the poor Indians' sake and the relief of future travelers to this country,
I could wish to stay here longer if we could do it in peace."*

– Narcissa Whitman
28 Nov. 1845

ORPHANS OF THE TRAIL

WHILE MARCUS WAS AWAY, various ailments had plagued Narcissa. Back at their mission, she slowly regained her health. They were certain that another summer would bring a fresh cavalcade of battered wagons from the East. The Whitmans planned on being ready to supply the newcomers with whatever they might need. They had no way of preparing for the challenges that were coming their way.

That fall of 1844, the Blue Mountains were beautifully hideous with snow. The struggle through the freezing passes was

1842

First U.S. wire suspension bridge, near Philadelphia, is completed.

January 6 –
In the Khyber Pass, in the rugged Hindu Kush, Afghans wipe out more than 16,000 British soldiers.

John Charles Frémont, *"the Pathfinder," scouts out and surveys parts of the West. He and his wife,* **Jessie Benton Frémont,** *will write a bestseller about what he sees and where he goes.*

just one more ordeal for one family's summer of disaster. Not long after little Catherine Sager fell under a wagon wheel and broke her leg, she and her brothers and sisters saw their parents become ill and die, one after the other, out on the Oregon Trail. Going by Mrs. Sager's last wish, folks on the wagon train took 10-year-old Catherine; John, 14; Frank, 12; Elizabeth, 8; Matilda Jane, 6; 3-year-old Louise; and baby Henrietta, 5 months old, to the mission at Waiilatpu. Years later, Catherine remembered gray-eyed Mrs. Whitman. With her "dark calico dress and gingham sunbonnet" she seemed to be "the prettiest woman we had ever seen."

The Sager orphans

1842

March 30 – Georgia – **Dr. Crawford W. Long** *is the first physician to offer ether, so a patient can sleep painlessly while being operated on.*

August 9 – The Maine-Canada border is finally settled.

On both sides of the ocean, ballrooms and parlors are full of polka dancers.

Narcissa wrote about them, too: "They were said to be very bad children," but no wonder – after what they'd been through. She promptly began shaping them up, teaching them, giving them Bible verses to memorize, and lining them up like a stairway, shortest to tallest, to sing for visitors. At first, young Frank Sager refused to put up with the Whitmans' strict household and ran away, but he soon returned. Waiilatpu became home for the Sager orphans. To them, Narcissa and Marcus became Mother and Father.

THE GREAT EXPERIMENT

THE SAGERS WERE JUST ONE FAMILY among the nearly 2,000 people who went West in 1844. More than double that number set out in 1845 as more and more U.S. citizens were embracing a huge, greedy, idealistic notion. In July 1845, journalist John L. O'Sullivan put the feeling in the land into words when he wrote

1843

December 12 – Volcanic eruption of Mount St. Helens (in modern-day state of Washington)	January 29 – **William McKinley**, future president, is born in Ohio.	**John James Audubon**, 58, is traveling this year, too, up the Missouri River to draw animals in the Wild West.		June – New York – Ex-slave **Isabella Baumfree** takes a new job: preacher; and new name: **Sojourner Truth**.

that it was Americans' "manifest destiny to overspread and to possess the whole of the continent which Providence has given us for the ... great experiment of liberty." This idea helped to fuel America's westward movement, ever pushing more and more native people from the lands of their ancestors. Loads of Americans were no longer content to share the Oregon Country with Britain as they had since 1818. They called for a firm line between British Canada and U.S. territory in the northwest, and they wanted it clear up by Alaska, at latitude 54°40'. The border would end up at the 49th parallel, but oh boy, in 1844, riled up people were shouting "Fifty-four Forty or Fight!" It was the campaign slogan for the winning presidential candidate that year, James K. Polk.

Less than a year after President Polk took office in 1845, the lone star of the Republic of Texas became one more spangle on the U.S. banner. Then, in 1846, U.S. soldiers went to war to take the rest of the West away from Mexico. Oh, yes, only 70 years after the Declaration of Independence, the United States was a juggernaut, a great unstoppable movement across the North American continent. Its people devoured books written by folks who'd seen the West. They gathered up courage and supplies, shook off rumors about illness (often true) and Indian attacks

1843

Dorothea Dix begins a 40-year campaign for humane treatment for mentally ill patients.

The preachings of **William Miller** lead tens of thousands of "Millerites" to sell all they have and look to the sky for **Jesus's** return to Earth in 1843 – 1844 at the latest.

November 10 – **John Trumbull**, 87, painter of the American Revolution, dies in New York.

(generally false), and hit the trail. Still, as blood-chilling news of the spectacularly unlucky Donner Party filtered its way back East, more than one American paused to think twice about taking on such a hard journey.

The Donner and Reed families of Springfield, Illinois, probably read Thomas Farnham's *Travels in the Great Western Prairie* (1843). They certainly studied Lansford Hastings' *The Emigrant's Guide to Oregon and California* (1845) and made its author famous – notorious, really – when they followed his travel directions. Hastings had been West. He'd even visited the Whitmans, but he never tried the California shortcut that he recommended in his book. He didn't know how oxen could die of thirst in the desert beyond the Great Salt Lake. Of the 87 men, women, and children in the "Donner Party," 35 starved and froze to death in the snowy Sierra Nevada mountains. More would have died if, as was reported, they hadn't eaten the dead bodies of their companions.

Still, the eastern emigrants kept coming and coming, crowding into the hunting lands of the Cayuse, Nez Perce, Flathead, and other native peoples. How would they and their horses live in their changing world with all of these newcomers

1844

Annapolis, MD – *The U.S. Naval Academy* *is founded.*	*June 26 –* Widower **President** **John Tyler** *marries* **Julia Gardiner.**	*Hit song: "Buffalo Girls* *(Won't You Come Out* *Tonight?),"* *by* **John** **Hodges,** *a.k.a.* **Cool** **White**
Charles Dickens *writes* A Christmas Carol.		

scaring off the game, hacking roads through the wilds for their wagons, and letting their animals eat all the grass? "The poor Indians are amazed at the overwhelming numbers of Americans coming into the country," Narcissa wrote to her folks, August 23, 1847. "They seem not to know what to make of it."

For their part, the "poor Indians" seemed to have made up their minds about Dr. Whitman and his proud wife who looked down her nose at them and wouldn't let them in *her* nice house on *their* land.

When traveling artist Paul Kane passed through, he sketched a pair of stern-looking men named Tilokaikt and Tomahas. Later, as Kane drew Marcus, he warned the missionary of the fury he had sensed among the Cayuse. Even the old White-headed Eagle, Dr. McLoughlin, who had welcomed the missionaries to Oregon, warned Marcus to leave Waiilatpu.

There'd even been trouble and smashed windows at the Spaldings' mission where Henry, Eliza and the Nez Perce had, for the most part, gotten along better than the Whitmans had with their neighbors. The Nez Perce were peaceful people and America's history would be quite different if members of this tribe hadn't kept Lewis and Clark and their crew of explorers

1844

June 27 – *Carthage, IL* – *An anti-Mormon mob murders* **Joseph Smith**. *Since the early 1830s, Mormons have been driven from one community after another (see 1847).*

January 10 – **Alexandre Dumas** *writes* The Three Musketeers.

J. M. W. Turner, *English artist, paints "Rain, Steam, and Speed."*

from starving to death back in 1805. But the changes in the 42 years since then had made Native Americans mad and fearful. Into this troubled land came a fresh wave of pioneers, all rash-spotted and fever-hot. Most of them would get to feeling better, but what if the Indians caught measles? That would be a different story. For many, that'd be the last straw.

MEASLES AND BLOOD

IT WAS COLD, GRAY NOVEMBER. Of the people at Waiilatpu – 70 or so, including emigrant families and the Whitmans' extended family – many were sick. Sick, too, were the Cayuse in their lodges not so far away. With Marcus's relentless doctoring, or in spite of it, the white folks slowly got well. Their immune systems knew how to fight measles. It was different for the men, women, and children of the Cayuse and other tribes. It didn't seem to matter what help

1845

May 22 – Washington, DC – **Samuel F. B. Morse** taps out the first telegraph message.

March 3 –
The Union adds Florida as the 27th state.

March 4 –
James K. Polk becomes the nation's 11th president.

A new law: From now on the U.S. election day is to be the first Monday in November.

they got from their *tewat* (medicine man) or Dr. Whitman. They still died. Young Catherine Sager reported seeing as many as six Cayuse buried every day. And that's not all she saw and heard. Not nearly all. She heard Marcus tell what the Cayuse were saying, that he was poisoning them so he could give their country to his people. She watched from her own sick bed as weary Marcus sat up through the night of November 28, 1847, keeping watch over the sick folks.

The next day was foggy. Some menfolk at the mission were working cattle in the dreary outdoors; it was butchering season. Narcissa was as gloomy as the weather that morning. Suddenly, her mood turned to terror at the sight of angry men in her kitchen, their fierce faces painted black and white. She shouted for Marcus, and in the next instant, he and the Cayuse were on one side of the bolted kitchen door with everyone else on the other.

Catherine Sager remembered "an explosion that seemed to shake the house."

A rifle shot! Angry voices!

"Oh, the Indians!" Narcissa screamed. "The Indians!" as the warriors ran outside.

A shot to the neck, tomahawk blows and slashes to his head

1845

July 4 – Massachusetts – So he could "live deep," and write a book about it, **Henry David Thoreau** *goes to live at Walden Pond.*

December 29 – *Texas becomes the 28th state in the Union.*

Edgar Allan Poe *writes* The Raven *and Other Poems.*

Nevermore!

Ireland — 1845–47 — *The potatoes are blighted. Crops fail. 750,000 people starve and die. Many, many more are leaving Ireland for America, forever.*

November 29, 1847: Day of fearful fury

and face had not killed him at first, but there was no way to save blood-drenched Marcus Whitman. In the next moment, Narcissa appeared at an upstairs window, where a bullet struck her.

Like her husband, she did not die immediately. She was

1846

May 13 —
U.S.-Mexican war begins. When it ends February 2, 1848, Mexico will be forced to accept $15 million for land which will become all or part of the U.S. states of California, Nevada, Utah, Texas, Colorado, Arizona, New Mexico, Wyoming, Oklahoma, and Kansas. Future Civil War generals of North and South fight side by side in the Mexican War.

New York City —
Alexander Cartwright *writes a set of rules for his new Knickerbocker Baseball Club.*

still alive when the Cayuse ordered one of the men, Andrew Rogers, to help carry her out of the mission house. Once outside, both he and Narcissa were shot dead. It's said that one of her killers lifted her head by its red-gold hair and hit her face, the face that had always seemed to the Cayuse so prideful and aloof whenever its owner looked their way.

Fourteen people died before the fury of killing was over, including Catherine's big brothers, 17-year-old John Sager and 15-year-old Frank. A black-robed Catholic priest came to the devastated mission by the Walla Walla and helped the survivors lay the victims to rest.

End of the trail

1846

June 14 – Bear Flag Revolt – American settlers, not knowing that Mexico and the U.S. are already at war, take over the Mexican fort at Sonoma and declare independence. A flag with a grizzly bear and a star proclaim a "California Republic."

Massachusetts – **Elias Howe** patents his invention: a practical sewing machine.

New Jersey – **Nancy Johnson** invents the hand-cranked ice-cream freezer.

Some people got away. A mom and dad and their little ones found a hiding place under the floor and escaped in the night, on foot, to Fort Walla Walla. After the killings, 6-year-old Louise Sager died of measles and a lack of good doctoring. So, eventually, did the mountain men's daughters, Helen Meek and Mary Ann Bridger, 10 and 11 years old. The only one who could talk to the Cayuse in their language was Henry and Eliza Spalding's daughter, a new student at the Whitmans' mission school. Later, her dad wrote that 10-year-old Eliza had to interpret for the Indians "till her voice failed from weakness ... [until she was] a mere skeleton, her mind as much injured as her health."

According to Catherine Sager, she, Eliza and more than 50 men, women, and children "were now captives of a horde of savages." Who could save them?

Edward Lear *writes*
A Book of Nonsense,
poems for children.

Illinois –
Abraham Lincoln
*gets elected to his one
term in the U.S. House
of Representatives.*

*The Smithsonian
Institution is founded
in Washington, DC.*

WAIILATPU

A CAYUSE CHIEF

The SPALDING Family

RANSOM

CAYUSE WAR

Worlds collide at the end of the Oregon Trail.

CHAPTER SIX

The World
They Left Behind

REVENGE

WHILE YOUNG ELIZA SPALDING was busy translating, some female prisoners were put to work sewing and knitting. With luck and her "teeth and nails," Catherine Sager managed to avoid what happened to three young women. They were taken away and made to act as wives by their captors. At last, after almost a month, the new superintendent at Fort Vancouver traded three boatloads of blankets, shirts, guns, tobacco, and such for the hostages' freedom. Even then, they barely escaped.

The furious Cayuse trashed, looted, and burned the buildings

1846

Italy –
Chemist **Ascanio Sobrero** discovers nitroglycerin, the main ingredient in **Albert Nobel's** 1867 invention: dynamite.

Artist **George Caleb Bingham** paints "The Jolly Flatboatman."

England –
John C. Horseley, pioneer greeting card artist, designs the first Christmas card.

at Waiilatpu. Wolves dug up the mass grave and scattered the bones of its people. Strands of Narcissa's hair drifted in the smoky wind. Joe Lafayette Meek, the frontiersman, mourned the death of his daughter, Helen. Eleven years earlier he had entertained Dr. Whitman's lighthearted bride with wilderness stories. Now he took on the job of carrying news of the Whitman massacre over the hard 3,000 miles to Washington, D.C.

Americans of 1848, who'd read the Whitmans' published letters and been encouraged by their journey, were horrified when they heard what had happened to them. The shocking news added to the buzz of an already remarkable year of popular uprisings and revolutions over in Europe. In New York, Elizabeth Cady Stanton had demanded female citizens' right to vote at the very first Women's Rights Convention. American men voted for a new president that year, too: General Zachary Taylor, hero of the Mexican War. Congress lost no time making Oregon Country an official U.S. territory, but all of this news faded as word of a glittering discovery on January 24, 1848, spread back East. Nothing made folks crazier and changed the West more than the rush for California gold.

But all of that was off in the unknowable future, meaningless

1846 **1847**

December 28 –
Iowa becomes the
29th state in
the Union.

Maine –
**Hanson Crockett
Gregory** *puts a hole in
the middle of a pastry
and invents the donut.*

*The U.S. Post Office
prints its first sticky
postage stamp. It costs
5¢ and has a picture of*
Benjamin Franklin
on it.

to the 300 furious men scrambling into Cayuse lands in 1848, ready for revenge and not much interested in whether or not any particular individual took part in the attacks on the missionaries. The angry militia swiped the Indians' horses and cattle and set their homes on fire. The Cayuse War, with its ugly raids and suffering, went on for two years until five men — Tilokaikt, Tomahas, Kiamasumpkin, Isiaasheluckas, and Clokomas — presented themselves for rough justice. After a rambunctious trial in Oregon City, a mob of people gathered to watch Joe Meek hang them, June 2, 1850. Folks say that before he died, Tilokaikt said this:

The last of Tilokaikt

"Did not your missionaries tell us that Christ died to save his people? So die we, to save our people."

Brigham Young *leads an exodus of Mormons to the valley of the Great Salt Lake.*

February 11 —
Thomas Alva Edison, *future inventor, is born in Ohio.*

Frederick Douglass *starts publishing the* North Star, *his anti-slavery newspaper.*

EPILOGUE

THE CHURCHMEN IN BOSTON were done with the Oregon project. Henry and Eliza Spalding and the other missionaries had to leave their posts. A big, sad deal is what it was, having to abandon work which was so important to them that they'd left behind just about every familiar thing and person in order to do it. Now the Spaldings and the others were pretty much like all the other Oregon pioneers: They were starting a new life.

It was finally too much for steely Mrs. Spalding, the *other* first woman from the United States to travel the Oregon Trail. Her health trickled away, and three years after Marcus and Narcissa were killed, 43-year-old Eliza was in a grave of her own. Henry Spalding lived until 1874, long enough to see most of his country's westward movement. Between his 1836 adventure and 1860, the year of the Pony Express, nearly 400,000 people went West.

1847

Massachusetts – **Esther A. Howland** *hires other women for her Valentine factory, one of America's first.*

March 3 – **Alexander Graham Bell**, *inventor of the telephone, is born in Scotland.*

Mexican War updates – April 18 – **General Winfield Scott** *leads the U.S. Army to a bloody victory at the Battle of Cerro Gordo.*

September 14 –
U.S. forces capture Mexico City.

Henry Spalding lived to see settlers jamming into the land where he and his wife and the Nez Perce had worked together. And in 1863, he saw his government doing its best to talk the peaceable Nez Perce out of all but the last of their territory. Dr. John McLoughlin, who'd helped so many newcomers, died broke in 1857, two years before Oregon became the 33rd state in a Union that was on the verge of Civil War. Now his statue as well as one of Dr. Marcus Whitman are in the U.S. Capitol, representing the states of Oregon and Washington.

Were Marcus and Narcissa Christian martyrs? Or were they and the Cayuse victims of misunderstandings and unintended consequences? Probably a little of this and a little of that.

In the end, Mrs. Whitman wanted to be a homemaker. Young Narcissa Prentiss had wanted to stand out, to do something extraordinary. While one might have advised the other to be careful what she prayed for, each had her prayers answered — in ways that she did not expect — at the end of the Oregon Trail.

July 26 – Africa – Liberians declare their independence from their colonial founders.

Charlotte Brontë *writes* Jane Eyre.

Emily Brontë *writes* Wuthering Heights.

William M. Thackeray *writes* Vanity Fair.

More
Information

Ezra Meeker

CHAMPION OF THE OREGON TRAIL

IT WAS 1852 WHEN YOUNG EZRA MEEKER went from Iowa with his wife, baby, and a couple of yokes of oxen to Oregon. He made and lost money in business and became the first mayor of Puyallup, Washington. Then, in 1906, white-bearded Ezra hitched a covered wagon to an ox team and headed East with a big idea: The Oregon Trail must be marked and remembered. All the way to Independence, Missouri, he painted inscriptions on markers and educated folks. He kept on going clear to Washington, D.C., where he and President Theodore Roosevelt talked about getting government money for permanent monuments. Ezra wrote books, founded the Oregon Trail Association, and in 1910 when he was 80, he again traveled the Trail by covered wagon. He made three more trips: by train, by car, and, in 1924, by plane — all in a single-handed effort to make sure that America's historic adventure on the trail to Oregon was never forgotten. Ezra Meeker was 97 when he died on December 3, 1928.

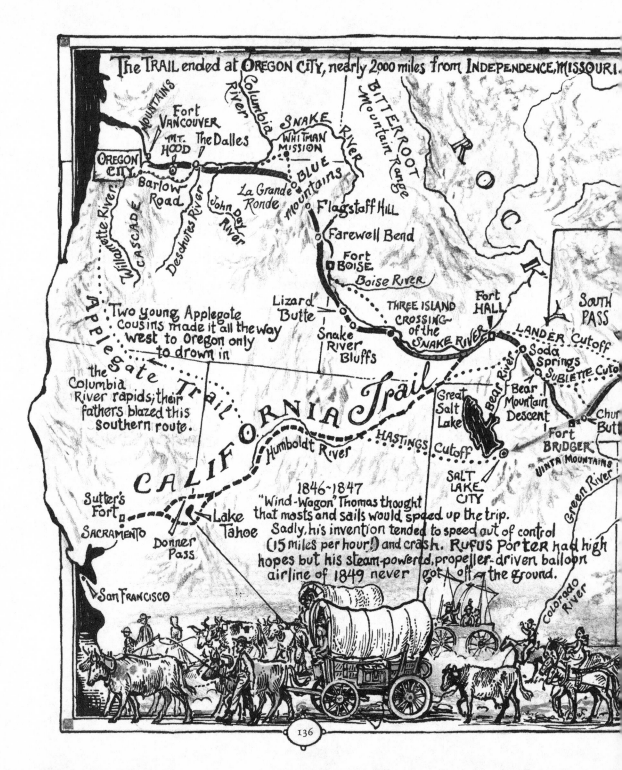

The TRAIL ended at OREGON CITY, nearly 2,000 miles from INDEPENDENCE, MISSOURI.

ROCKY Mountains

BITTERROOT Mountain Range

SNAKE River

Columbia River

Fort VANCOUVER

The Dalles

MT. HOOD

OREGON CITY

Barlow Road

CASCADE Mountains

Willamette River

Deschutes River

John Day River

La Grande Ronde

BLUE Mountains

WHITMAN MISSION

Flagstaff Hill

Farewell Bend

Fort BOISE

Boise River

SOUTH PASS

LANDER Cutoff

Lizard Butte

THREE ISLAND CROSSING of the SNAKE RIVER

Fort HALL

Snake River Bluffs

Soda Springs

SUBLETTE Cutoff

Bear River

Applegate Trail

Two young Applegate cousins made it all the way west to Oregon only to drown in the Columbia River rapids; their fathers blazed this southern route.

CALIFORNIA Trail

Humboldt River

HASTINGS Cutoff

Great Salt Lake

Bear Mountain Descent

Fort BRIDGER

Church Butte

UINTA Mountains

Green River

Sutter's Fort

SACRAMENTO

Donner Pass

Lake Tahoe

SALT LAKE CITY

1846-1847 "Wind-Wagon" Thomas thought that masts and sails would speed up the trip. Sadly, his invention tended to speed out of control (15 miles per hour!) and crash. Rufus Porter had high hopes but his steam-powered, propeller-driven balloon airline of 1849 never got off the ground.

San Francisco

Colorado River

136

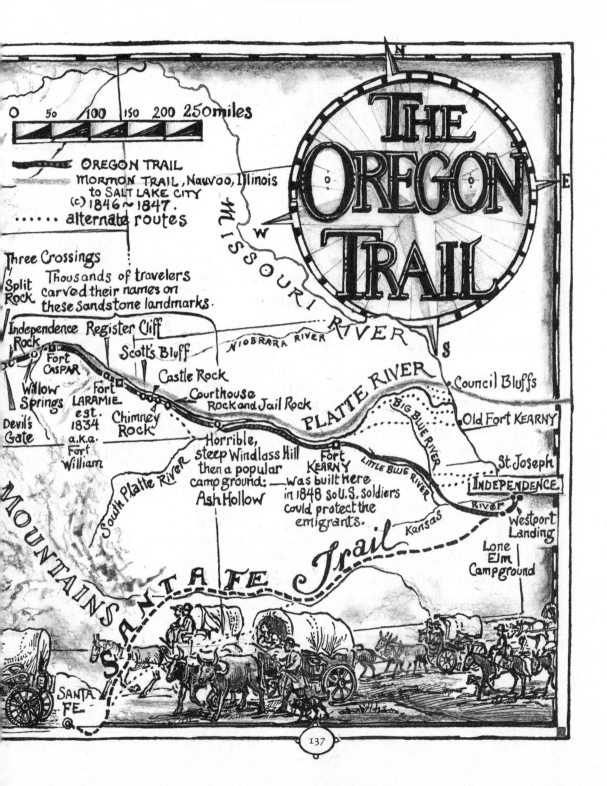

THE OREGON TRAIL

O 50 100 150 200 250 miles

— OREGON TRAIL
MORMON TRAIL, Nauvoo, Illinois
to SALT LAKE CITY
(c) 1846~1847.
······ alternate routes

Three Crossings
Split Rock

Thousands of travelers carved their names on these sandstone landmarks.

Independence Rock
Register Cliff
Scott's Bluff
Castle Rock
Courthouse Rock and Jail Rock
Fort CASPAR
Willow Springs
Fort LARAMIE est. 1834 a.k.a. Fort William
Chimney Rock
Devil's Gate

MISSOURI RIVER
NIOBRARA RIVER
PLATTE RIVER
South Platte River
BIG BLUE RIVER
LITTLE BLUE RIVER

Council Bluffs
Old Fort KEARNY
St. Joseph
INDEPENDENCE

Horrible, steep Windlass Hill then a popular camp ground: Ash Hollow

Fort KEARNY was built here in 1848 so U.S. soldiers could protect the emigrants.

Kansas River
Westport Landing
Lone Elm Campground

SANTA FE Trail

MOUNTAINS

SANTA FE

OREGON TRAIL CHRONOLOGY

1804 – 1806 Lewis & Clark Expedition to the Pacific Northwest

1811 In Oregon, John Jacob Astor founds Astoria, a fur-trading post and first American settlement west of the Rocky Mountains.

1812 – 1813 From the Columbia River in the west to Missouri in the east, Robert Stuart and other Astorians traverse in reverse what will become the Oregon Trail. They discover the South Pass, principal passageway through the Rockies.

Feb. 13, 1822 William Henry Ashley puts a trapper want ad in the *St. Louis Gazette*. The men and boys who reply will be the greatest generation of real-life, legendary mountain men, explorers, and guides in the old, Wild West.

1825 The first fur traders' rendezvous is held in Wyoming.

1830 Wheels roll West as Jedediah Smith, Bill Sublette, and David Jackson lead a caravan of supply wagons to the Rocky Mountain rendezvous.

1836 Narcissa Whitman and Eliza Spalding are the first female U.S. citizens to travel the length of what would become known as the Oregon Trail.

1841 John Bidwell and John Bartleson co-captain the first true wagon train to Oregon and California. Ex-trappers Joe Meek and Tom Fitzpatrick are guides, or "pilots."

1842 Lieutenant John C. "Pathfinder" Frémont and Kit Carson explore the Rocky Mountains.

112 people strike out across the Oregon Trail.

1843 The "Great Emigration": As many as 1,000 pioneers demonstrate that wagon travel West is real, and "Oregon Fever" sweeps the country.

Settlers on the Willamette River form a provisional government in Oregon. Oregon City is its first capital.

Frémont leads another exploring, mapmaking expedition, this time pressing on to Oregon. His *Topographical Map of the Road from Missouri to Oregon* is a bestseller.

1844 Nearly 2,000 people leave for Oregon.

Overlanders begin using a shortcut on the Oregon Trail known as the Sublette Cutoff.

1845 More than 5,000 overlanders travel on the Trail this year.

Sam Barlow and Joel Palmer hack out an overland route to bypass the deadly Columbia River rapids. Pioneers pay a toll to travel the horrid Barlow Road. It beats drowning.

1847 The year begins with news of the Donner Party tragedy and ends with that of the Whitman massacre. Shocking.

Midwestern Mormons begin migrating to Salt Lake City, Utah.

1848 Gold is discovered in California, and Oregon becomes a U.S. territory.

1849 U.S. soldiers begin guarding travelers on the Oregon Trail.

1849 – 1853 Almost a quarter of a million travelers seeking gold and land crowd the Oregon/California Trail. Cholera epidemics kill thousands.

Sept. 9, 1850 California becomes the 31st state.

1850 U.S. Congress passes the Donation Land Law. Any male citizen over 18 settling in Oregon before December 1850 can receive 320 acres of land. So can his wife.

1852 In this peak year for America's westward movement, 10,000 pioneers head for Oregon; 60,000 go to Utah or California.

Aug. 19, 1854 Near Fort Laramie, in present-day Wyoming, a clash over a settler's cow leads to a deadly battle between U.S. soldiers and Brulé Sioux people. This "Grattan Massacre" leads to nasty raids back and forth until the Sioux are finally, cruelly put down at the Battle of Wounded Knee, South Dakota, in December 1890.

Feb. 14, 1859 Oregon becomes the 33rd state.

April 3, 1860 U.S. mail is carried by Pony Express from St. Joseph, Missouri, to Sacramento, California, until October 24, 1861, when telegraph lines are connected across the West.

May 10, 1869 The transcontinental railroad is completed, but well into the 20th century, dwindling numbers of wagons will still roll along the Oregon Trail.

Resources

BIBLIOGRAPHY

Carlson, Laurie Winn. *On Sidesaddles to Heaven*. Caldwell, ID: Caxton Press, 1998.

Drury, Clifford M. *Marcus and Narcissa Whitman and the Opening of Old Oregon*.
Seattle, Washington: Northwest Interpretive Association, 1986.
(The Drury book has many quotes from Marcus.)

Franzwa, Gregory M. *The Oregon Trail Revisited*. Tucson, AZ: Patrice Press, 1997.

Hill, William E. *The Oregon Trail, Yesterday and Today*. Caldwell, ID: Caxton Press, 2000.

Jeffrey, Julie Roy. *Converting the West: A Biography of Narcissa Whitman*.
Norman, OK: University of Oklahoma Press, 1991.

Mattes, Merrill J. *The Great Platte River Road*. Nebraska Historical Society, 1969.

Olson, Steven P. *The Oregon Trail: A Primary Source History of the Route to the American West*.
New York: Rosen Publishing Group, Inc., 2004.

Tunis, Edwin. *Frontier Living*. New York: HarperCollinsPublshers, 1961.

Unruh, John. *The Plains Across: The Overland Emigrants and the Trans-Mississippi West, 1840–1860*.
Chicago, IL: University of Illinois Press, 1979.

Uschan, Michael V. *The Oregon Trail*. Milwaukee, Wisconsin: World Almanac Library, 2004.

Ward, Geoffrey C. *The West*. Boston, MA: Little, Brown and Company, 1996.

Whitman, Narcissa. *The Writings of Narcissa Whitman*. Fairfield, WA: Ye Galleon Press, 2002.
(This book includes several letters written by Marcus, too.)

RECOMMENDED FOR YOUNG READERS

Blackwood, Gary L. *Life on the Oregon Trail*. San Diego, CA: Lucent Publishing, 1999.

Erickson, Paul. *Daily Life in a Covered Wagon*. Washington, DC.: The Preservation Press, 1994.

Fisher, Leonard Everett. *The Oregon Trail*. New York: Holiday House, 1990.

Isaacs, Sally Senzell. *The Oregon Trail*. Chicago, IL: Heinemann Library, 2004.

Legay, Gilbert. *Atlas of Indians of North America*. Hauppauge, NY: Barron's Educational Series, Inc., 1995.

Stefoff, Rebecca. *Children of the Westward Trail*. Brookfield, CN: The Millbrook Press, 1996.

Thompson, Gare. *Our Journey West*. Washington DC: National Geographic Society, 2002.

Walker, Paul Robert. *True Tales of the Wild West*. Washington DC: National Geographic Society, 2002.

PLACES WELL WORTH VISITING

National Frontier Trails Museum, 318 West Pacific, Independence, MO 64050 •
816.325.7575 • www.ci.independence.mo.us/NFTM/

Western Historic Trails Center, 3434 Richard Downing Ave., Council Bluffs, IA 51501 • 712.366.4900 •
www.state.ia.us/iowahistory/sites/western_trails/western_trails.html

Stuhr Museum of the Prairie Pioneer, 3133 West Highway 34, Grand Island, NE 68801•
308.385.5316 • www.stuhrmuseum.org

Chimney Rock National Historic Site, P.O. Box F, Bayard, NE 69334 • 308.586.2581 • www.nps.gov/chro/

Fort Laramie National Historic Site, 965 Gray Rocks Rd., Fort Laramie, WY 82212 • 307.837.2221 • www.nps.gov/fola/

Whitman Mission National Historic Site, 328 Whitman Mission Road, Walla Walla, WA 99362 •
509.522.6357 • www.nps.gov/whmi

Oregon Trail Foundation, 1726 Washington St., Oregon City, OR 97045 • 503.657.9336 • www.endoftheoregontrail.org

www.americanwest.com/trails/pages/oretrail.htm • Special feature on the Oregon Trail on the American West Web site

www.octa-trails.org • The Oregon California Trails Association's excellent Web site

THE PICTURES

Here I sit in my upstairs studio in Independence, Missouri, the "Queen City of the Trails," as I try my best
to envision what things were like hereabouts when this place was all muddy and bustling with canvas-topped wagons.
It's a stretch, seeing as I can be at the airport in an hour and in Portland, Oregon, by nightfall.
Ah well. All sorts of reference books help, especially those with pictures made by eyewitnesses Paul Kane,
George Catlin, and that more recent, brilliant author/illustrator, Edwin Tunis. As artists have done for many a year,
I wedge a steel pen point into its wooden holder then dip it into a bottle of India ink again and again
until all of the pictures are drawn. I shade them with pencil and lamp black watercolor.

THE WORDS

Luckily, Narcissa Prentiss Whitman as well many of her countrymen were fine letter writers and journal keepers.
They knew that their lives were part of a great historic adventure. Then and ever since,
it was a time well worth documenting. And, too, for those courageous pioneers, their only connection
with their far away dear ones (and with us) were words on paper. Thanks to them, we here in their
unimaginable future can get an idea about what their world was like.
It was tough, and it's an honor to try to explain it.

My goal here, as in all of the books I have done and those that will be done, God willing, is a lively story
about those who are gone, faithful and true to their memory.

Index

ACKNOWLEDGMENTS
I wish to thank Mr. Richard Edwards of the National Frontier Trails Museum and Mr. Roger Trick of the Whitman Mission National Historic Site for their assistance, and I continue to be grateful for the reference librarians at the Mid-Continent Public Library. This book is dedicated to them.

Book design by David M. Seager. Design production by Ruthie Thompson, Thunderhill Graphics.
Text is set in Celestia Antiqua. Display type is Celestia Inline.

For information about special discounts for bulk purchases,
please contact National Geographic books Special Sales: ngspecsales@ngs.org.

Library of Congress Cataloging-in-Publication Data
Harness, Cheryl.
The tragic tale of Narcissa Whitman and a faithful history of the Oregon Trail / written and illustrated by Cheryl Harness.
p. cm.
ISBN-10: 0-7922-5920-3; ISBN-13: 978-07922-5920-6 (hardcover)
ISBN-10: 0-7922-5921-1; ISBN-13: 978-0-7922-5921-3 (library binding)

1. Whitman, Narcissa Prentiss, 1808–1847—Juvenile literature. 2. Women pioneers—Oregon National Historic Trail—Biography—Juvenile literature. 3. Women missionaries—Oregon National Historic Trail—Biography—Juvenile literature. 4. Frontier and pioneer life—Oregon National Historic Trail—Juvenile literature. 5. Oregon National Historic Trail—History—Juvenile literature. 6. Overland journeys to the Pacific—Juvenile literature. 7. Oregon—History—To 1859—Juvenile literature. 8. Oregon—Biography—Juvenile literature. I. Title.
F880.H275 2006
917.804'20922-dc22

200503093

Printed in the United States of America